Rights
to
Responsibility

Rights
to
Responsibility

Multiple Approaches
to Developing
Character and Community

Alanda Greene

Zephyr
Press ©

REACHING THEIR HIGHEST POTENTIAL
Tucson, Arizona

Rights to Responsibility
Multiple Approaches to Developing Character and Community

Grades 4–9

© 1997 by Zephyr Press
Printed in the United States of America

ISBN 1-56976-039-X

Editors: Stacey Lynn and Stacey Shropshire
Cover design: Stirling Crebbs
Design and production: Daniel Miedaner
Typesetting: Daniel Miedaner

Zephyr Press
P.O. Box 66006
Tucson, AZ 85728-6006

Library of Congress Cataloging-in-Publication Data

Greene, Alanda, 1947-
    Rights to responsibility : multiple approaches to developing
character and community / Alanda Greene.
        p.   cm.
    Includes bibliographical references.
    IBSN 1-56976-039-X
    1. Social ethics—Study and teaching—Activity programs. 2. Human
rights—Study and teaching—Activity programs. 3. Civics—Study and
teaching—Activity programs. 4. Environmental responsibility—Study
and teaching—Activity programs. 5. Moral education.   I. Title.
    HM216.G587 1996
    303.3'72—dc20   96-25421

Contents

Contents

Introduction

Considered from the perspective of recorded history, the idea of human rights is a recent concept. Although most countries in the world adopted the United Nation's International *Declaration of Human Rights* in 1949 and have acknowledged these rights in principle, in practice there is much ground to cover to enact these rights in the lives of all humans. But the ideal, the vision, has been named and has provided a reference point, a standard from which to assess situations. It is a goal for which to strive.

More recently, the United Nations adopted the *Declaration of the Rights of the Child* in 1959 in recognition of the special status of children. The concept of children's rights expanded in the years following this declaration, and in 1989 the UN General Assembly unanimously adopted the Convention on the Rights of the Child. As countries sign this convention and move to ratify it as law, the ideas contained in it actualize, move from concept to reality. An important dimension of actualization is widespread public awareness of the ideas.

Even more recent is the idea of rights for living things other than humans, and for Earth itself and the various dimensions of it. This concept, too, is growing. As visions of the future emerge, it becomes clearer that the future of humans and the future of the planet are tied together—the health and vitality of one is the health and vitality of the other.

As we continue to understand rights, responsibility is also clarified. From responsibility emerges empowerment—a sense of both belonging and contributing.

Experts commonly acknowledge that we are in a crisis. Many have referred to the nineties as "the turnaround decade," when the choices humans make will determine whether damage done and being done to Earth—the soil, water, air, living creatures—can be turned, rectified, redressed. If such rectification happens, it will happen because there are human beings who care for themselves, one another, and Earth; who are capable and willing to act on their caring; who believe that their actions matter both personally and in the community; who are aware of the issues facing Earth; and who can face these issues without giving in to hopelessness, helplessness, despair, or cynicism. These characteristics must be fostered in our youth.

As these ideas take shape in the minds of the world's children, they influence choices, directions, expectations, and visions of the future. But the potential in these ideas can become a potent force only if we are aware of them. For this knowledge to inspire and guide action, it must be internalized, digested, absorbed, and felt.

I have designed the activities in this book to contribute to this process, to engage students actively in learning about the concepts of human rights and responsibilities, the rights of all Earth, and the deep connectedness shared between humans and nature. The book employs a variety of learning strategies, allowing for many ways to respond to learning, process information, and express understanding. Research into how the brain works and how learning is best enhanced has established that humans have many ways of learning and knowing, many kinds of intelligence. When learning and understanding can be internalized in a variety of ways—with word, image, music, movement, gesture, and number—knowledge becomes meaningful, rich, and personal.

Using This Book

Cooperative Learning Groups

Many activities in this book ask students to work in small learning groups, usually of three to five people. Cooperative groups are gaining wide acceptance as a learning strategy, increasingly complementing more familiar individual and competitive approaches used in the classroom. Cooperative groups are an effective tool and can enhance learning significantly when used appropriately. This strategy requires specific techniques and applications; it is much more than just putting kids together in groups and carrying on in the same way that we conduct lessons geared to individuals.

I organized the activities with the expectation that teacher and students would be familiar with basic ideas about working in cooperative groups. If your students or you have had no experience with such groups, I suggest a workshop, in-service, or one of the many books available (for example, one of several by Johnson and Johnson). When you acquire a deep understanding of this learning strategy and practice it, you will be able to conduct the activities successfully. You may still use all activities with the class.

> ### Basic Expectations for Cooperative Groups
> ◆ *offer ideas*
> ◆ *stay with the group*
> ◆ *be involved*
> ◆ *listen to one another*
> ◆ *take turns*
> ◆ *speak kindly*
> ◆ *move in close*
> ◆ *keep your voice with your group*

If you or your students are familiar with learning in cooperative groups, I suggest you review some basic expectations.

Useful ways to reinforce these expectations include the following:

Posters

A classroom poster clearly listing the expectations for behavior in cooperative groups will be helpful. You can refer to it if students exhibit behaviors contrary to those listed (and they will, of course, since the skills of working in groups take time to learn).

The students can generate an equally helpful poster titled "Working in Groups: What Works, What Doesn't." Making this poster will require students to have some experience in small-group work so they will understand effective and ineffective group behavior. Such a classroom poster is useful when students behave inappropriately; you can direct their attention to the poster. When they are the ones who have generated the list, they more easily accept reminders about it.

Self-Assessment

You can easily adapt the group expectations to self-assessment (see the following forms). Give copies to students to complete at the conclusion of each lesson; the assessments will provide ongoing reminders and reviews of the skills necessary for working effectively with others.

Group Member's Evaluation

Name: _____

Project: _____

Date: _____

Members of Group: _____

_____

After each question, mark a line on the continuum that reflects the appropriate response to the question.

How would you rate the overall performance of the group?

Low _____ High

How would you rate your own performance?

Low _____ High

Who listened well? _____

How did they show they were listening well? _____

_____

_____

Who contributed? _____

Who didn't? _____

Did everyone stay on task? _____

_____

_____

Group Evaluation

Project: _____

Date: _____

Group Members: _____

_____

How well did we do the following?

Offer ideas?	rarely ____	sometimes ____	usually ____
Stay with the group?	rarely ____	sometimes ____	usually ____
Get involved?	rarely ____	sometimes ____	usually ____
Listen to one another?	rarely ____	sometimes ____	usually ____
Speak kindly?	rarely ____	sometimes ____	usually ____
Get close?	rarely ____	sometimes ____	usually ____

What really helped our group was _____

_____

Next time we will improve our group work by _____

_____

_____

_____

_____

Group Evaluation

Project: _____

Name: _____

Group Members: _____

_____

What behaviors helped your group? _____

_____

_____

What behaviors did not help? _____

_____

_____

Who contributed helpfully? How? _____

_____

_____

Who could have been more helpful? How? _____

_____

_____

List three things you will do next time to improve your performance:

_____

_____

_____

Assessment, Evaluation, and Reporting

What we value in the classroom, we evaluate. If we teach and expect behaviors such as those listed for working in cooperative groups, but the criteria for determining grades and marks on report cards are numerical test scores only, we deliver a message that behavior doesn't really count. Therefore, finding ways to include these expected behaviors in the assessment and reporting process strengthens the message that these are important, that they are valued, which requires a process of systematically observing and recording behaviors.

One of the benefits of cooperative group learning is that the teacher doesn't have to be center stage; the teaching role can expand. There is more opportunity to observe students working and interacting with others. Using a checklist or other simple assessment form, you can monitor behaviors over time.

Group Discussion in Cooperative Learning

Many of the activities ask that students discuss ideas in small and large groups. It is important that students have an understanding about these discussions, that students feel comfortable with having various points of view in the group, that students appreciate the richness of varied opinion.

Discussions are important parts of the activities, allowing students to begin to clarify their present beliefs (for beliefs change over time) and to discover more clearly what is important to them. At the same time, the activities provide opportunities for students to hear other points of view and consider other perspectives.

Much learning takes place through discussion. It is often through this process that what we really think and feel about an issue becomes clear in our minds.

Encourage discussion, then, but with appropriate noise control. If students aren't familiar with the small-group format for discussion, some may find it difficult to keep to the topic and control their volume. With feedback, assessment, and reflection, however, the awareness and desired behavior will come. Sometimes it takes students a while to realize that their own thoughts and feelings are being asked for and are genuinely valued. Many children still come from environments where they have little opportunity to express their own ideas or where they

Symbols Used to Record Behavior

↙ going off task

← leaving the group

ⱱⱱ disrupting behavior

Ⓣ dominating

X̱ not listening

☹ stating put-downs (words, tone)

↗ keeping directed, on task; helping group to focus

☺ praising, encouraging

✓ giving ideas, suggestions

? asking questions; developing meaning

∞ working close, face to face

Name of Student	Assignment or Project Date			

Sample Evaluation Using Process Skills

Evaluation

Subject: _____

Name: _____ Date: _____

Activities:

In the last month students have participated in a variety of learning activities about Japan. They have watched slides and videos, taken notes, discussed ideas in small groups, made a chart that compared leisure time in Japan with that in their own country, created—as a group assignment—a symbol system and a map of Japan showing growing and producing areas.

Evaluation for this period is as follows:

group work: (keeping on task, contributing ideas
　　　　　and effort, working positively,
　　　　　avoiding distracting behavior) ....50 points

chart (complete, accurate, neatly done) ....15 points
map (complete, accurate, neatly done) ....15 points
notes (thorough, legible, organized) ....20 points
tests and quizzes...30 points

TOTAL 　...130 points
Class average .... _____

have no one who listens. And our methods of teaching often give the message, not verbally but structurally, that children have nothing worthwhile to contribute and that the best thing they can do is accept what is taught. If we are committed to encouraging students to value their own and one another's thoughts and feelings, we need to give them the opportunity to exhibit this behavior. If the behavior is new, the students and teachers may need to relearn.

Reflective Journals

Many activities that follow include questions or statements for personal reflection. These questions are usually at the end of an activity, after students have had an opportunity to discuss and explore a concept.

Individual students will write these reflections and will not necessarily share them with the group. A workbook or journal where students' private ideas can be recorded over time is a valuable resource for students and teacher to observe growth and increased understanding. The reflective journals are also an excellent resource for creative writing and discussion ideas.

Brainstorming

Some of the activities ask students to brainstorm ideas. If students are not familiar with this process, spend time before the activity and cover the expectations for brainstorming. The most important aspect of this technique is to bypass the censoring, judging part of the mind and let ideas flow freely, which is how creative insights are reached.

What brainstorming means is that many of the ideas generated won't be used in the end; students may blurt out ideas that seemingly have no application or connection to the topic, and the judging mind may want to call them silly. But let them come. Often these ideas lead to other, helpful associations, or they provide a connection to another idea that emerges three thoughts further on.

Criticizing the ideas of others can readily shut down the risking, exploring part of a person's mind, can suggest that to avoid hurt, people have to keep their ideas in the safe and normal zone. But this kind of thinking isn't what we want to encourage in young people, so it's important to emphasize these brainstorming procedures.

Brainstorm Process

- All ideas are accepted.
- No ideas are criticized or made fun of.
- Ideas aren't edited or changed.
- Ideas can be repeated.
- Similar ideas can be stated.
- As many ideas as can be are generated.
- Ideas can build on other ideas, or piggyback.

Reaching Consensus

In some activities, students are asked to reach a decision as a group, or come to a consensus. Without practice in proper group behavior, students may adopt undesirable strategies to achieve consensus, ranging from dominating the conversation and the opinions of others through verbal fluency to dominating by volume or other bullying tactics to voting on the issue. Reaching consensus isn't any of these.

Reaching consensus requires that every person contribute views and that the group reach an outcome with which everyone can live. It doesn't necessarily mean full agreement and it doesn't mean the majority gets its way. It evolves through discussion; through clarifying ideas, views, and wording; through giving and taking.

Points on Consensus Process

- Clearly identify the focus of the decision making, that is, what is to be decided.
- Listen to all ideas; everyone has an equal voice; respect each voice.
- Consider all views.
- Ask questions; communicate feelings; contribute ideas.
- Listen, listen, listen.
- Accept that it takes time to reach a decision through consensus.

Circle Sessions in the Classroom

A circle session is a structured opportunity for communication. Participants sit in a circle, which enables each person to see everyone in the group and creates a sense of unity or shared purpose.

Regular use of circle sessions has been shown to greatly enhance language arts skills, beginning with speaking and listening, later extending to reading and writing. Participants develop awareness of and a vocabulary for describing feelings, thoughts, and behaviors, and increase their understanding of the relationship among social interactions, thoughts, and feelings.

Circle sessions encourage students to become more aware of what they are feeling, which is an important contribution to their education. Being unaware of one's feelings or the feelings of others has been identified as a significant characteristic of those suffering psychological problems later in life. A growing number of health professionals count ignored or repressed feelings as significant factors in many diseases such as cancer, stroke, and arthritis.

Students must adhere to certain guidelines if circle sessions are to be effective.

Circle Session Guidelines

- Everyone has a turn.
- A person may choose to skip a turn.
- What's said in the circle stays in the circle.
- Everyone listens to the speaker, which means looking at the speaker, avoiding fidgeting or distracting behavior, and avoiding talking out of turn.
- No one puts down or gossips about anyone else.
- Participants sit in a close circle.
- Participants have time to learn the guidelines well.

Establishing clear rules and sticking to them allows circle sessions to be an effective tool in the classroom, improving social climate and creating a more caring classroom community (a natural offshoot of the process). Ideally, circles should be held every day: as a way of bringing everyone together in the morning, after recess, or at the start of the afternoon.

The process is simple. Create a circle, welcome each student by name to the circle, and give a topic. Students have a few moments to think over the topic, each person indicates if he or she wishes to share (crossing hands in the lap is more relaxed, less insistent and distracting than hands up), participants speak only once, everyone has an opportunity for observation and comment, and everyone is thanked for participation regardless of whether the person spoke or not.

The simplicity of the process can belie the value of circle sessions. You may be tempted to skip the welcome or closing parts, which can seem contrived or artificial. You may be tempted to elicit more "profound" insights from students or provide the insights if students don't seem to have grasped what you wanted them to learn.

Avoid these temptations; trust and use the circles, stick to the guidelines, and observe the results. Topics that are good for beginning sessions to build trust while learning the procedure include the following:

- One of my best holidays
- One of my favorite places
- A happy memory
- Something I'm looking forward to
- Things I enjoy learning
- Someone who trusts me
- A favorite book (animal, movie, food, sport, music)
- A scary dream
- If I could be anything I wanted

Sometimes students will attempt to sensationalize or exaggerate, or tell something to get a reaction. It's important to accept what is said without judgment, whether it seems a very "nice" thing and the temptation is to give praise, or whether something that seems reprehensible is shared, tempting reprimand or displeasure. When the anticipated reaction doesn't happen, sensationalizing quickly ends.

However, sometimes something more serious is revealed in a circle session. It's wise to warn children ahead of time, when you are explaining the guidelines, that if they reveal something that is against the law or threatens their well-being, the law requires you to investigate or take action. Usually if a student makes such a revelation, it is likely a call for help or intervention. If you have agreed that what is said in the circle stays in the circle, this situation can be challenging. In my classes it has rarely happened, but when it does, I have spoken with the child privately and received permission to pursue the incident further. You can then act without compromising one of the guidelines. Remember, however, that with or without their permission, you must report the incident.

Welcoming participants at the start of the circle and thanking them at the close may seen contrived or awkward, but it provides benefits that make it worthwhile to persevere until it feels natural. A sense of beginning and end, a sense of inclusion, and a sense of seriousness all result from the consistent use of this very simple procedure.

When all students who wish to contribute have done so, ask students what they observed or learned. What similarities or patterns did they notice? What did they learn about themselves? Did they have any insights? This part of the circle session is very important; it emphasizes that the process is a learning activity and that learning can take place in different ways. Hearing other people's responses and observations often clues or triggers the awareness that a similar response is taking place within ourselves.

Personal Journal

Following the circle session, give students the chance to respond privately to one of the following questions: What did I learn in the circle session? What did I learn about myself? What insights did I have?

In the beginning, some students may have difficulty expressing or acknowledging feelings, or they may state only that they feel "fine" about an incident that you think would evoke strong emotional involvement. If a person has had no experience in identifying feelings or in having the chance to name and express them, learning to do so will take some time. The time will be well spent and the result is worth waiting for, however.

You can conduct circle sessions using any of the topics provided in the activities, then have students reflect on the topics in their personal journals. Thus you develop circle session skills in the context of this unit of study.

Drama in the Classroom

Teachers often avoid drama activities in the classroom for many reasons: lack of space, noise, low amount of perceived learning for the time spent, loss of control as students get "wired up" and hard to bring to focus, difficulty maintaining discipline, and discomfort from not knowing where to begin or how to approach it. Many schools include little or no drama as part of the regular learning, so many of us never acquired that background.

However, drama activities have much to recommend their use: learners become involved and interested, students have opportunities to experiment with various roles, the feeling dimension is included, students are engaged, few or no materials are required, students are given opportunities to be creative, and learners are responsible for much of the content.

The first few experiences with drama may indeed result in excessive noise and perhaps unanticipated discipline problems, especially when it's time for students to settle down and focus. I have found that learners are enthusiastic and willing to participate in these activities, however, and adjust to the expectations quite quickly. Establish expected behaviors from the start, which, if you have a small room, may include that students rehearse in whispers in small groups around the room.

Most important, drama is a powerful learning tool. As learners act out and feel the various roles they create and portray, they have a chance to experiment with and experience various interpretations and perspectives. Drama provides an opportunity to develop speaking and listening skills in a meaningful context. And it makes learning fun.

Many good resources exist for introducing drama into the classroom, which usually contain introductory activities for building awareness and becoming familiar with expectations and routines. These simple games can allow students to be more relaxed and confident with new learning situations, and with creating skits or acting out created situations.

Exploring Rights

In this activity students work with the understanding and knowledge they already have, which allows their own experience to be validated, establishes a context into which new knowledge can be integrated, and helps clarify for the teacher the nature and extent of the students' understanding.

▶ **Structure**

class, small groups, and individuals

▶ **Material**

paper

pencils *(activity book)*

large paper for each group

reflective journal

▶ **Time**

1 class period *(30 to 40 minutes)*

▶ **Procedure**

Step 1: With the class, ask the question, "What is a right?" and elicit several responses. Accept all ideas; clarify that a right is something to which one is entitled (usually having the backing of law, but not always). Ask for examples of rights; accept whatever is offered at this time. The purpose is to generate ideas and stimulate connections, not get "a right answer."

Step 2: Working individually, students list in their workbooks, in journals, or on paper as many examples of rights that they can think of. Ask them to record examples of rights they personally have.

Step 3: In small groups, students share in turn the rights they have listed so far. They brainstorm a list of as many rights as they can think of. Students then discuss to reach a consensus of what they feel are the ten most important rights on their lists. The designated recorder writes down the ten items for each group under the heading "Declaration of Rights."

Step 4: The reporter for each group reads aloud to the class the list of ten rights selected and then posts them where everyone can see them. When every group's list has been read aloud and posted, the class examines all the declarations and notes the common items. Ask the students to comment on any patterns they notice in the lists, any new thoughts or insights they have had since seeing and hearing all the rights presented.

Step 5: Working individually in their reflective journals, students complete the following phrase: *I personally consider the most important right to be _____ _____ because . . .*

Declaration of the Rights of the Child

When the United Nations adopted the *Declaration of the Rights of the Child* on November 20, 1959, they approved ten principles to acknowledge that the child requires special safeguards and care beyond the rights and freedoms set forth in the Universal Declaration of Human Rights.

Thirty years later, the General Assembly of the United Nations unanimously voted to adopt the *Convention on the Rights of the Child.* This document contains 54 articles, a considerable elaboration on the principles of the 1959 document, describing in more detail the responsibilities and duties of the state toward the child, as well as the inherent rights of the child.

Because the ten principles of the declaration are accessible and useful, I have used them for the following activities.

▶ Structure

same groups as for activity 1

▶ Material

2 copies of *Declaration of the Rights of the Child* for each group

paper

reflective journals

copies of ten rights from activity 1

▶ **Time**

1 class period (*30 to 40 minutes*)

▶ **Procedure**

Step 1: Pass out the first copies of the United Nations' *Declaration of the Rights of the Child*. Explain that it is a significant document of this century. Tell students that after experiencing the horror of the Second World War, many people were moved to create basic protection for all people in the world. The *International Declaration of Human Rights* was adopted by all members of the United Nations on December 10, 1948. December 10 is observed worldwide as Human Rights Day.

Many people felt that children were in a special category and needed extra care and protection during their growing years. (The document defines a child as anyone under the age of 18.) The *Declaration of the Rights of the Child* was written and all countries of the United Nations adopted it. Much needs to be done to ensure all children in the world have these rights.

Step 2: In the same groups as in the preceding activity, students examine the ten rights they generated in activity 1 and compare them to the ten rights in the *Declaration of the Rights of the Child*.

Write the following four questions on a chart or the chalkboard and ask the groups to record their responses to them.

1. What rights, if any, are in the UN document and your document? (The wording doesn't have to be exact, but the meaning or idea should be there.)

2. What rights are in your document but not the UN's document?

3. What rights are in the UN's document but not your document?

4. After reading through and comparing both documents, record any changes your group would make to either document (adding, subtracting, altering, replacing any existing rights).

Step 3: A reporter from each group reads aloud to the class the group's comparisons and changes. Invite questions and discussions.

Step 4: Cut the second copies of the UN *Declaration of the Rights of the Child* into ten strips, one right per strip. Ask students to place the strips in the center of their group and, while discussing the rights, to rearrange the strips so that what the students consider most important is on top and least important is on bottom. Students may place some strips side by side.

Have students tape or glue the strips to a separate piece of paper with the three most important at the top, the three least important at the bottom.

Step 5: A reporter from each group reads aloud to the class the group's selections of most and least important rights. Invite questions and discussion.

The process of selecting some of the rights as more important than others may challenge students, encouraging deeper thought about and examination of the meaning of *right*. At the end of this activity, emphasize that all rights are equally important, that the activity was meant to stimulate discussion and thought. You may find sometimes that some students are flippant or seem uncaring about these rights, and you may note responses or comments that suggest shallow thinking. You may be tempted to think your students are not mature enough for the activities. However, persevere. Students often have not been asked to think deeply about such issues. They have been told what is right. This material also may be very new and students may not have had sufficient time to internalize and understand some of the implications. Keep at it, however, and appreciate the understanding that does deepen over time.

Step 6: Working individually in response journals, students copy and complete the following statement: *If I had to eliminate all but three rights from the UN* Declaration of the Rights of the Child, *these are the rights . . .*

I chose these rights because . . .

UNITED NATIONS DECLARATION
of the Rights of the Child

- The right to affection, love, and understanding

- The right to adequate nutrition and medical care

- The right to free education

- The right to full opportunity for play and recreation

- The right to a name and nationality

- The right to special care, if handicapped

- The right to be among the first to receive relief in times of disaster

- The right to be a useful member of society and to develop individual abilities

- The right to be brought up in a spirit of peace and universal brotherhood

- The right to enjoy these rights, regardless of race, color, sex, religion, national or social origin

Rights and Responsibilities: Part 1

The Personal Rights Reflection work sheet is to be completed by students individually; it can provide topics for sharing in a circle session format. Review the section on using circle sessions (pages 13–15).

▶ **Structure**

small groups and class

▶ **Material**

1 copy of song lyrics for each group

1 copy of UN *Declaration of Rights of the Child* for each group

1 copy of original list of ten rights from activity 1

1 copy for each student of Rights and Responsibilities work sheet

1 copy for each student of the Personal Rights Reflection work sheet

▶ **Time**

1 to 2 class periods *(30 to 40 minutes each)*

▶ Procedure

Step 1: Distribute one copy of song "I Have a Right" and UN *Declaration of the Rights of the Child* to each group. The lyrics contain the ideas from the UN declaration in different wording.

Step 2: Ask the groups to read the lyrics and match a right from the declaration with a phrase or line from the song. Record any rights that are not identified or suggested in the lyrics. Record any ideas or rights named in the lyrics that are not identified in the declaration (for example, responsibility).

Step 3: Have students examine the third verse of the song. Have groups discuss the following question: How are rights and responsibilities connected? Have them summarize main ideas and record them.

Step 4: Read the summary from each small group to the class. Identify similarities and discuss key points.

Step 5: Ask students to examine their list of rights from activity 1.

Each student is to identify and record on the Rights and Responsibilities work sheet (on page 29) one or more responsibilities that go with each right that is listed, as in the following example:

The right to privacy.
I have the responsibility to respect other people's privacy.

Students keep this work sheet in their response journals or activity books.

Step 6: Invite students to share with the class examples of rights and accompanying responsibilities. Record students' examples on a large chart. Post it in a visible place.

Step 7: Working individually in their response journals, students complete the following statements.

Rights and responsibilities are connected because . . .
The right that is most important to me is . . .
The responsibility that is most important to me is . . .

Step 8: Working individually, each student completes the Personal Rights Reflection sheet.

I Have a Right

words and music by Alanda Greene

I Have a Right

I have a right—to a name that is my own.
I have a right—to a country and a home.
I have a right—to a place where I belong.
I have a right to love.

Chorus:
And if I know these rights are for me,
I also know they're for everybody.
And with them comes responsibility
To honor the rights of everybody.
And I understand, I can clearly see
We all have a right to love.

I have a right—to play and learn and grow.
I have a right—to protection, and I know
I have a right—to comfort, kindness, care.
I have a right to love.

Chorus

I have a right—to be the best that I can be.
I have a right—to use my ability.
I have a right—to live in a world of peace.
I have a right to love.

Chorus

Rights and Responsibilities

This is a right that I have	This is a responsibility that goes with it

Personal Rights Reflection:
How My Rights Are Respected

Name:_____

My home is like this: _____

My country is _____

People I love are _____

_____

_____

_____

Ways and things with which I like to play are_____

_____

_____

_____

Ways and things I like to learn are _____

_____

_____

_____

Ways I am protected are _____

_____

_____

_____

Some goals I have are _____

_____

_____

_____

Abilities I have and ways I want to develop are _____

_____

_____

_____

_____

A time I was given comfort was _____

_____

_____

_____

Ways others have shown caring to me are _____

_____

_____

_____

Ways I have shown caring are _____

_____

_____

_____

My idea of a world of peace is _____

_____

_____

_____

_____

Rights and Responsibilities: Part 2

▶ **Structure**

small groups

▶ **Material**

chart of Rights and Responsibilities from previous lesson

▶ **Time**

1 class period (*30 to 40 minutes*)

▶ **Procedure**

Step 1: Ask each small group to select a pair of the rights and responsibilities from the list created and posted in the previous activity.

Step 2: Have students create a small skit or other piece of drama that involves all group members and that shows a situation in which someone isn't acting with responsibility about a particular right. You may extend the example concerning the responsibility to respect the privacy of others to clarify your expectations. For example, students could enact an older brother or sister finding a younger sibling's diary while looking for something. The older one reads some pages in the diary and then teases the younger one, threatening to tell other people.

Step 3: After discussing, creating, rehearsing, and refining the skits, each group performs its skit for the class.

Step 4: After each group has presented its skit, a member asks the audience to identify which posted right has not been respected and to explain the disrespectful behavior.

Step 5: After identifying the right and responsibility, the performing group asks members of the audience to suggest how the person whose right was not respected could respond appropriately. How could the person speak up for his or her rights and let the other person know that the action was irresponsible?

Step 6: Students respond individually to the following questions in their journals: Describe a time when someone didn't respect your rights, or describe a time when you didn't respect another person's rights. What happened as a result?

A Time When Someone Did Not Respect My Right

▶ **Structure**

circle session: 1 large circle or 2 smaller circles that run consecutively (*1 group works at a quiet task while the other meets in a circle session; then the groups switch.*)

▶ **Material**

▶ **Time**

15 to 20 minutes (*You will need more time the first time you do a circle session since you will need to explain the expectations and guidelines.*)

▶ **Procedure**

Step 1: Clearly teach the guidelines for circle sessions (see pages 13–15).

Step 2: Introduce the topic.

Step 3: Instruct participants to focus on describing the action or the event and to avoid naming people. Include an instruction to note feelings and possible feelings. To help students you may need to ask them what they felt during the situation, how they felt afterward, and how they feel now.

Step 4: After each person who wants to has contributed, ask what similarities students noticed in the responses. Did anyone learn anything? Inquire as to what similarities students noticed and what they learned from the responses.

A Time When I Did Not Respect Someone Else's Right

Just as it is important for children to be able to express wrongs they perceive done to them, it is also important for them to have the chance to admit when they acted inappropriately. It is also important that they discuss their feelings about the topic.

▶ **Structure**

same as in activity 5

▶ **Material**

▶ **Time**

same as in activity 5

▶ **Procedure**

Step 1: Clearly teach the guidelines for circle sessions (see pages 13–15), if you have not already done so.

Step 2: Introduce the topic.

Step 3: Instruct participants to focus on describing the action or the event and to avoid naming people. Include an instruction to note feelings and possible feelings. To help students you may need to ask them what they felt during the situation, how they felt afterward, and how they feel now.

Step 4: After each person who wants to has contributed, ask what similarities students noticed in the responses. Did anyone learn anything? Inquire as to what similarities students noticed and what they learned from the responses.

Current Events and Human Rights

In the previous activities, students have opportunities to explore the idea primarily of personal rights and responsibilities. This activity allows students to expand their understanding by examining the abuses of children's rights in current worldwide situations.

▶ **Structure**

individuals and class

▶ **Material**

1 copy of UN declaration, posted in the classroom or accessible to each student

world map or atlas

1 evaluation form for each student

▶ **Time**

several days before activity for students to collect sufficient information

1 class period *(30 to 40 minutes)* for presentation and discussion

▶ **Procedure**

Step 1: Several days before this activity, ask students to investigate news sources for stories indicating that children's rights have been violated in some way.

Encourage students to select from a variety of print and nonprint sources. This activity is a good opportunity for students to use periodical research skills.

Step 2: Also give each student a copy of the evaluation form. Ask them to keep it and complete it after they present their research to the class. Explain to them that their presentations will be evaluated according to the criteria described in points 1, 2, and 3 of the form. Both the student and the teacher will complete an evaluation of the student's presentation. You may modify the sample evaluation form (page 41) to suit your needs. On the form provided, a score of 9/10 would indicate a well-met criterion, and 5/10 would indicate that a fair amount of information was missing.

Step 3: Each student is responsible for bringing at least one print and one nonprint example of a violation. Using the UN declaration, each student identifies which right or rights have been violated in each situation.

Step 4: Using the world map or an atlas, ask students to locate the place where their events occur.

Step 5: Each student orally presents the two news pieces to the class, telling which right has been violated and indicating on the world map where this event took place.

Step 6: Invite student comment and exploration about responsibility in connection to the violation of these rights. Where does responsibility lie? With whom? Is there any evidence of people who are acting responsibly? Encourage exploration of these questions. Sitting in a circle is a helpful way to encourage involvement and contribution of ideas. (Not all classrooms lend themselves to moving easily into a circle format, however, so if only a few minutes' discussion is likely to occur, moving into a circle may be too disruptive or time consuming.)

Step 7: After all students have given their presentations, have them complete the following statements in their personal journals:

The story I found most interesting, moving, sad, or troublesome is . . .

because . . .

I think that this situation could be improved by . . .

Step 8: Students complete and turn in the evaluation form.

Child Rights and Current Events
Examples of Violations

Information collected and presented by _____

Date: _____

Student Evaluation

1. I accurately and clearly explained the information.

   I included accurate names of people and places.

   I correctly identified the area on the map. .... /10

2. I clearly identified the rights that were violated.

   I clearly explained the way in which the right
   was violated. .... /10

3. I spoke clearly, looked at the audience, and spoke in
   an appropriate volume and at an appropriate speed. .... /5

Teacher Evaluation

1. You clearly and accurately explained the information.

   You included accurate names of people and places.

   You correctly identified the area on a map. .... /10

2. You clearly identified the rights that were violated.
   You clearly explained the way in which the right
   was violated. .... /10

3. You spoke clearly, looked at the audience, and
   spoke in an appropriate volume and at an
   appropriate speed. .... /5

Making a Poster

Expressing ideas in images can be a powerful way to internalize understanding, especially for those children who tend to process ideas visually. The strong visual appeal of posters makes them a valuable way to display student learning in the classroom, in the hallway, or in local areas of the community.

▶ **Structure**

individuals

▶ **Material**

poster paper *(Bristol board or manilla tag)*

pencil crayons, paint, or felt crayons

paper and pencil for preliminary ideas and rough sketches

> *Note: I prefer pencil crayons to felt ones, since felts often stain other posters if the posters are stacked. Pencil crayons also allow students to control the intensity of color and allow more variety and contrast.*

▶ **Time**

2 or 3 class periods for most students *(The time needed to complete a project like this varies greatly from individual to individual. After you have given class time, allow a few more days for students to complete the assignment at home or in spare school time.)*

▶ Procedure

Step 1: Review the purpose of a poster, which is to communicate information quickly and to attract the attention of a passerby. Posters need not have words on them. If students use words, they should be clear and easy to read, and should convey information quickly. If possible, bring examples of posters to display, which you can find easily in the art reference section of your school resource center.

Step 2: Display the "Criteria for Effective Posters" (page 44). These ideas serve very nicely for evaluation. Provide each student with a copy of the information and the expectation that both student and teacher will evaluate the finished work according to these criteria.

Step 3: Ask students to select one of the rights listed in the UN *Declaration of the Rights of the Child* and to communicate an idea about this right on a poster. The right can be written on the poster if the student wishes.

Step 4: After roughly working out ideas, students prepare posters using the posted criteria.

Step 5: When all students have completed their posters, display the posters. Note which rights have been represented, the different ways in which rights have been presented, and the effective ways of communicating with a poster.

Step 6: Have students work individually in their personal journals to complete the following sentences:

I chose _____
as the right to express in my poster because . . .

One thing I especially like about my poster is . . .

One thing I might do differently if I did my poster again is . . .

Something effective I noticed in another poster was . . .

Criteria for Effective Posters

Balance: The lettering and images should be balanced evenly on the page, not crammed or concentrated in one area only.

Unity: The elements of the poster—lettering, pictures, color—should have a sense of belonging together, rather than being a collection of isolated elements put on a page. Using techniques such as overlapping of images and words, a color theme, and connecting images can help achieve a sense of unity. Isolated and disconnected elements on the page can take away from a sense of unity.

Contrast: Contrast is achieved primarily through choice of color, as well as through shape and design, with the purpose of making important information stand out clearly. Placing bright colors next to dull colors creates contrast; placing strong colors next to soft colors creates contrast.

Theme: The images and words used should support the purpose of the poster and the information, message, or idea it is communicating.

Border: In most cases the elements should not come right to the edge of the paper. A border isn't always necessary, but a definite surrounding space is effective.

Lettering: If lettering is used, the main words should be clear and easy to read, as should all information on the poster.

Quality: The poster should have a sense of completeness. It should look as though the creator applied a sense of thought, planning, and sustained work to it. It should be neat, carefully designed, and finished.

Rights to Responsibility © 1997 Zephyr Press, Tucson, Arizona

Poster Evaluation

Name: _____ Date: _____

Theme: _____

Poster Criteria	Student Evaluation	Teacher Evaluation
Balance	/5	/5
Unity	/5	/5
Contrast	/5	/5
Theme	/15	/15
Border, Lettering	/5	/5
Quality	/15	/15
TOTAL	/50	/50

Student Comments

Something I really like about this poster is _____

_____

_____

_____

Suggestions:_____

_____

_____

_____

Teacher Comments

Something I really like about this poster is _____

_____

_____

_____

Suggestions:_____

_____

_____

_____

What Others Have Done; What I Can Do

Through participation in the previous activities, students have been involved in many ways with ideas and feelings concerning the rights of children. Offering opportunities to express their learnings, wonderings, and feelings in various ways is important. In addition to encouraging articulation and providing a process to clarify thoughts and feelings, writing provides another way to evaluate, to assess learning to date, and to determine appropriate additional learning experiences.

▶ **Structure**

individuals

▶ **Material**

paper

pens or pencils

resource center for research

▶ **Time**

2 or more class periods

▶ **Procedure**

Step 1: Review as a class what you have learned so far about the rights of children, about responsibility to respect these rights, and about violation of rights; review students' concerns or questions.

Step 2: Invite students to give names of people or organizations who have worked for the rights of children. (Well-known groups include UNICEF, Red Cross, Amnesty International, Save the Children Fund, CARE, and Oxfam.)

Step 3: Ask students to select one organization and research some of its accomplishments and efforts with children's rights. Students may choose one particular person within the organization or research the organization itself. Each student is responsible for collecting the information, organizing it, and writing a short article that describes the accomplishments. This process includes making a rough draft, revising (which may include pairing with another student to share and discuss ideas), editing (which may also include small-group or paired involvement), and drafting a final copy.

Step 4: Invite students to express their personal ideas of how they can responsibly contribute to the protection of children's rights. Encourage them to consider a wide range of opportunities, from home to community to nation to world. In what ways do students feel they can have and do have the desire to make a contribution? Have students develop a final draft as described in step 3.

Step 5: When students have completed the writing, allow students to read their works aloud to the class. Sharing written expression is an important dimension of writing, and the information about various organizations also contributes to the learning of the group.

Step 6: Give each student a copy of the evaluation form (page 48). Ask students to complete the form and turn it in with their final drafts.

Child Rights:
What Others Have Done; What I Can Do

Research and writing prepared by _____

Date: _____

I researched, made notes, and collected information about this
organization: _____

1. I expressed the information I learned in my own
   words and clearly described how this organization
   or a person within it has helped children, including
   what children's rights they supported. .... /15

2. I expressed my own ideas about how I could
   contribute to respecting children's rights. .... /15

3. I organized my writing so that my ideas are
   expressed with order, relationship, and clarity .... /15

4. I edited my work so that spelling, capital letters,
   punctuation, and sentence structure are according
   to standard usage. My final copy is neat and complete. .... /15

What I would like noticed about this piece of writing is

_____

_____

_____

Teacher

What I noticed about this piece of writing is _____

_____

_____

_____

_____

Rights to Responsibility © 1997 Zephyr Press, Tucson, Arizona

Where Do I Stand?

This activity asks students to literally take a position. Create a large space in your classroom by moving desks, tables, and chairs against the walls, or use a gym or outside area. Mark two lines far apart enough for everyone in the class to be able to choose a position between them. Designate one line "totally agree" and the other "totally disagree."

This activity presents a good context for discussing the pressure to conform to the majority view. It also encourages exploration of gray areas, areas where a right or wrong answer is not always evident. This dimension is important to include. Many consider the degree to which a person can tolerate ambiguity to be a significant indicator of mental health. As the rate of change in the world accelerates, the ability to adjust and reconsider prior learnings is a necessary skill. In addition, as societies become increasingly multicultural and people are exposed to increasingly varied social norms and values, the ability to accept a range of responses on an issue contributes to building tolerant, peaceful communities.

You may use this activity at the beginning of a class, if the room easily accommodates it, and deal with only one situation at a time, following with a short discussion. Alternatively, explore several situations during one class, discussing each after students have taken their various stands. Allow students ample opportunity to question, respond, explain, and adjust their positions in a friendly atmosphere that emphasizes clarification and increased understanding. Discourage any approach that criticizes, denigrates, or insults another person's stand.

Remind students frequently that they have a right to take their own stands, which may differ from those of others. It is also fine for them to change position when, through thoughtful discussion and reflection, they achieve a new understanding about a position. It is interesting to observe students listening to someone's reason for taking a particular position and adjusting their own stand as a result of what they hear.

Controversial situations arise frequently in communities, in the news, and in daily living. Encourage students to think of such issues from their own lives to use in this activity. Be alert to current situations from newspapers, magazines, television, and radio. The activity allows students to engage thoughtfully, yet in a safe context, with the relevant issues of their daily lives.

▶ Procedure

Students begin by standing between the two lines. Read a situation aloud and ask that students individually find positions somewhere between the poles that represent their stands on the issue.

Situations

1. A store owner has had difficulty with shoplifters. Several times a week a group of young people come into his store and create distractions. When they leave, many items are missing from the store. He hasn't been able to catch anyone, as there are too many people for him to be able to watch all of them. He is getting frustrated. This day he sees a group of young people coming toward the store. He goes into the street, and tells them they are not welcome in his store and to go away. One of the youths hollers at him, "I have a right to come into your store. You have no right to stop me." What is your stand regarding the youth's statements?

2. Wu Lee's family emigrated from their homeland before he was born and now live in a neighborhood with many other people of the same race. Often people from races different from his insult him, even though he is as much a citizen as they are. He feels angry when he is insulted. One day at school he sees a girl wearing a T-shirt with a slogan making fun of his race. He confronts her and angrily tells her she has no right to wear that shirt. She tells him she has a right to wear whatever she wants. What is your stand on the girl's position?

3. Angelo has a favorite hat that he wears almost everywhere. The hat has an ad for a well-known beer on it. Mr. Davidson is Angelo's social studies teacher. He has forbidden Angelo to wear the hat in class because he thinks it promotes drinking. The social studies class is studying the dangers to young people of using alcohol. Mr. Davidson says that to allow Angelo to wear the hat in class would be hypocritical. Angelo says his rights are being violated. What is your position on what Mr. Davidson says?

4. Mohan Singh lives in Canada and practices the Sikh religion. When he became old enough, he decided to be formally baptized into the Sikh faith, which means he will observe certain practices all his life. These practices include not cutting his hair (which he keeps under a turban) and wearing a *kirpan*, or ceremonial dagger, at all times. It is forbidden to bring weapons of any kind onto Mohan's school grounds. He says his rights to practice his religion are being violated. Where do you stand on whether he should be allowed to wear his *kirpan*?

5. In some places in the world such as Sweden, it is against the law to spank or strike a child. In other places, people consider spanking to be a way to teach children that some things are inappropriate. Some people feel it is a necessary part of learning right from wrong. What is your position on spanking (or hitting) as a form of discipline?

6. A young girl was supposed to be home by 9 o'clock at night. One evening, she was with a group of girls and didn't pay attention to the time. She arrived home at 9:40 P.M. Her father was furious and struck her several times, giving her a black eye. What is your position on his action?

7. Miguel's grandmother takes care of him during the week while his parents work in a city some distance away. Miguel is required to do his share of the household chores every day, which include washing the

supper dishes, making his bed, and carrying out the compost. He has neglected these tasks for several days. His grandmother says he is grounded for the weekend. He tells her she has no right to limit his freedom. What is your stand on what Miguel says?

8. Jacinta is a thirteen-year-old girl who lives on an island in Papua New Guinea. Her father is a soldier in the army. The government has ordered the army to arrest anyone belonging to a certain revolutionary group who oppose the government and are trying to establish their own country. The rebels who are caught are put in jail and sometimes tortured. Jacinta's father told her these rebels are trying to destroy their country by breaking it up and they must be stopped. He instructs her to tell him if she suspects any of the families of her friends at school to be rebels. Jacinta knows that the brother of her best friend is part of the revolutionary group. She likes him and doesn't want him to get into trouble. She doesn't want to let her father know but feels bad about disobeying him. In Jacinta's culture, it is considered very important for children to obey their parents. Jacinta hasn't said anything to her father yet. What is your stand regarding Jacinta's right to keep silent?

9. Every evening Megan talks with her friends on the telephone. Her mother is concerned that Megan's school grades have dropped recently and wonders if her friends are having a bad influence on her performance at school. Megan discovers that on this evening her mother has been listening to her conversation on an extension. She is upset and tells her mother, "You have no right to invade my privacy." Megan's mother replies that, since Megan lives in her home and she supports Megan and is responsible for Megan's welfare, she has a right to know what Megan is doing in order to be able to protect Megan from possible bad influences. What is your stand on Megan's mother's action?

10. Maria and Stacey spend a lot of time at school and on weekends with a group of good friends. Others at school like them and their teachers and parents respect them. A new girl has moved to their area and is in their classes at school. Maria has heard that this girl was in a lot of trouble at her previous school. She dresses roughly and looks tough. Stacey has talked with her and seems attracted to her. Stacey says the new girl is exciting and different; Stacey wants to include her in some of their activities. Maria says including her will give them a bad reputation and people will think they are just like the new girl. Stacey says that they don't have a right to judge her based on how she used to be. Maria says it's better to be safe than sorry. What is your stand in relation to Maria's position?

11. Farid lives in a small fishing community near the ocean. Several years ago a man moved there, bought a home, opened a small store, and became a well-known person in the town. He was very helpful to many people on different occasions and did a lot of volunteer work with different groups. He has coached hockey for two years and also gives free swimming lessons in the summer. A few weeks ago the people in the community learned that this man was once convicted for child molestation. Now many community members say he is unfit to work with children or be around them. They want him to leave their community. Farid is glad to finally have a hockey coach and doesn't think they have a right to prevent the man from coaching; if the man made a mistake, he's paid for it. No one has a right to keep him from doing this community work. What is your position on the community's opinion?

12. Rabia is a fourteen-year-old girl who lives in Montreal. Her family came to Canada from Syria and all of her family are Muslim. Rabia has given much thought to her religion and feels now that she wants

to practice it more fully, to really live according to the teachings given in the Islam holy book, the Koran. As part of her religion, she chooses to wear a *hijab,* or head covering, sometimes called a veil, whenever she goes anywhere in public. When she began wearing the hijab to school, however, her school principal told her that she was not allowed to wear it because it represents the oppression and restriction that women of the Islam faith are forced to live under. It has no place in a world where women are struggling to gain equal rights and to be able to express their freedom. Rabia claims that she has chosen to wear the veil freely and has a right to do so. Where do you stand on the principal's decision?

Town Hall Meeting

This issue is the low-level flight testing of military airplanes in the tundra near Goose Bay, Labrador. Various groups are interested in influencing the decision on whether the number of flights increases, stays as it is, or ceases.

In this activity, students play members of interest groups attending a town hall meeting. An effective way for you to be part of the group and give effective feedback is to play a member of the media. Students take turns presenting their views about the issue from the perspectives of the roles they are playing. The situation represents the clashes between different rights and allows students to experience some sense of the difficulty of determining which rights will be given priority.

If students need feedback, the presider can call the meeting to a close to reconvene the next day (which could be in a few minutes), and someone can read the local reporter's notes aloud. Such a strategy allows the teacher to communicate about points that are not being considered, groups who are not effectively getting their message across, or domination tactics being used by a particular group, without interrupting the role-play.

If you wish, give students time to research key concepts and concerns about this issue in the school or local library. Areas to consider are the effects of loud noise on health, the effects on tundra wildlife, the purpose of low-level flight testing, and the lifestyle of the Innu, the aboriginal people who live in that region.

One way to organize students into groups is to cut out enough squares of different colored paper, one color for each group, to divide the class evenly. Each student draws a piece of paper out of a container and belongs to the group designated by that color.

▶ Time

2 class periods

▶ Procedure

Step 1: Using the colored paper strategy or another random strategy, place students in the following groups: wildlife biologists, military personnel, town residents, health officials, Innu, and Citizens for a Safe Planet. In addition, select someone to chair the meeting, and include the press (if desired).

Step 2: Copy the descriptions of the interest groups and pass them out to the appropriate groups. Allow students time to meet and discuss their position before proceeding. If you are giving students time to research, they should do so now.

Step 3: Bring students together in a circle. The chair of the meeting keeps the meeting in order, keeps track of the order of speakers with one person speaking at a time, and makes sure various groups have a chance to speak.

Step 4: After students have discussed the issue and students have presented and defended their various points of view, assign students to new groups so they take new positions and present their views from another perspective.

Step 5: After completing the town hall meetings, ask students to complete the following phrases in their journals, expressing their own thoughts and feelings rather than those of the roles they were playing:

What I learned from this activity was . . .

What I found difficult in this activity was . . .

Interest Groups

Military

Various North American and European nations pay to use this air space for the testing of low-level flights. Low-level flights allow planes to escape radar detection. These tests allow fighter pilots to be trained in the procedure. Such tests require a flat terrain without obstruction and a large area. Few such places exist in the world. Such flights in this area have numbered more than 9,000 yearly, but NATO (North Atlantic Treaty Organization) has possible plans to develop a training base for flight testing by member nations in Europe and North America. These plans could more than double the yearly flight tests in the region.

Health Concerns

Differing opinions exist about the effect of loud noise on health. Some medical officials claim that loud noise is related to birth defects, including effects on the hearing of unborn children. Young children and the elderly are especially sensitive to loud noise. It seems to increase blood pressure and heart problems. At least one doctor claims that no evidence exists to show that this kind of loud noise causes ear damage or hearing loss.

Native Peoples

Many Innu people claim that flight testing disturbs the regional wildlife and affects their traditional way of life. Caribou migration patterns are disturbed as are other wildlife behaviors. More important to some Innu, who call this land *Nittasinan*, is the claim that it is their ancestral land and was never ceded to the Canadian government. The government therefore has no right to be there at all. They feel that their culture and way of life are threatened by the flight testing by what are essentially foreign nations on their land.

Wildlife Biologists

Many biologists note that no study has been done to assess the effect of this noise on surrounding wildlife. There are, for example, songbirds in the region who have very thin skulls, which could easily be damaged by loud noise. These birds depend on hearing for their survival. They have no economic value, but their survival and that of other animals should be considered before tests continue, and possible effects on their well-being should be researched.

Residents of Goose Bay

The flight testing brings in almost all the money that supports this town. Without the flight testing, the town would not survive. The people need the income provided by the testing. Many people live here. They want to keep their work. They would not be able to sell their homes if they had to leave. They say that it is noisy, but "You get used to it."

Citizens for a Safe Planet

This community group claims that military flight testing encourages increased development of weapons and moves in the direction of war. Some of the training is a practice for a possible nuclear strike. No one should be practicing for a nuclear war. If the planet is to become one of peace, then its people and nations must make an effort in that direction, which means that low-level flight testing to allow undetected attacks on another country should not be allowed.

Evaluation: Town Hall Meeting
Flight Testing in the Tundra

Name: _____ Date: _____

First Role: _____

Second Role: _____

After each criterion, mark a line on the continuum that reflects the quality of the performance.

Presented point of view clearly and expressed reasons for holding this point of view.	**Student** weak _____ strong **Teacher** weak _____ strong
Listened to the ideas of others, considered them, and responded thoughtfully when appropriate.	**Student** weak _____ strong **Teacher** weak _____ strong
Behaved respectfully by listening as others spoke, without distractions or out-of-turn talking.	**Student** weak _____ strong **Teacher** weak _____ strong
Maintained role through the exercise.	**Student** weak _____ strong **Teacher** weak _____ strong

In Another's Shoes

This activity allows students to learn a little about how the goodwill of others affects the lives of individual children. It asks students to imagine (and to build a context for that imagining) what it would be like to be a child whose rights have not been acknowledged or met. How would it feel to experience the goodwill of people who do care?

Step 1: Copy the personal stories, which are written as if told by an actual person who has experienced the benefits and aid offered through an organization. Although the stories are fictional, they are built from the testimonies and accounts of actual events and experiences that children have described or others have described witnessing. Following each story is a brief description of the appropriate organization and its work.

Step 2: After students have heard or read the stories and descriptions, have each choose an organization and imagine that he or she is a child whose rights are not met in some way. Have them create imaginary lives and then describe how their lives would change as a result of the organization. The organization that a student chooses, of course, sets the scene for the life the student chooses to imagine.

Step 3: You may choose to give them time to research their organizations so they can choose an appropriate environment or situation.

Step 4: Students write their ideas and descriptions from the point of view of the person who has the experience—an autobiographical story.

Step 5: Students recount this story to the class, as if the student were the person telling another group what he or she has experienced. When students tell their stories, they develop the voices and characters of the people they created beyond what occurs merely by writing the stories.

Some students may find this activity too challenging, depending on their degree of confidence in and experience speaking dramatically to the class. If it appears so difficult and demanding that students would not have a positive learning experience, encourage them to work in pairs. Two students can tell the story as if both people had a common experience. This technique provides support and the security of someone standing with the student, which is often enough for students to overcome shyness, to make the experience valuable and accessible.

Personal Stories

1. My name is Barbara. I ended up on the streets in Toronto when I was fourteen, after I ran away from home. Sometimes when I was panhandling on some corner, a person would ask me what I was doing. "Why don't you go home?" an older man said to me one day, like I was just being some kind of selfish, ungrateful brat.

   Living at home became impossible when my mother started living with Jack. She couldn't or wouldn't hear what I was talking about when I tried to tell her that I couldn't stand him around, that he really bothered me. I knew she loved him— more than she did me, that's for sure—and as long as he was there, there was no place for me in that house. One night he came home late again. He'd been drinking, and I knew he'd be coming to my bedroom just like before. I just grabbed my coat and headed out the door and I haven't been back since. That was more than six months ago.

   I knew there were kids like me who had run away and were living on the streets, so I headed downtown to places where I'd seen them. I never thought the life would be so cruel, though. I thought maybe that having had whatever kind of life had made them run away, they'd be more understanding or kind. I met some good people, but mostly it got pretty scary.

There's lots of drugs and violence on the street. You can't trust anyone. This guy Ben was really generous to lots of kids at first. He got them to use stuff really cheap, talked about how it made you feel better. Then people got hooked, and Ben raised his prices. Where can you get that kind of money on the street? What choices do you have? Like I said, I was panhandling. I didn't want to use drugs, but there's lots of pressure. People don't trust you if you don't. And you have to give some of what you get panhandling to these "bosses" who control different sections of the street. If you work in their area, you have to pay them. If you don't, you get hurt bad.

I'd been hanging out with a group. A few of them were pretty good, a bit scared maybe like I was. You start to think you have no place to go, like no one will want you anymore. The street bosses tell you that, too. "You can never leave the streets," Ben would say. Anyway, one night this guy named Mike—he was only about thirteen I think—got beat up bad by a gang from another area. He was bleeding bad and I figured he was going to die. They just left him there on the street. No one seemed to care. I was really scared and just stood there watching from across the street. Someone must have called an ambulance because one came and took him away. I was watching and wondering if the same thing was going to happen to me, when a young woman came and stood beside me. She said her name was Carole, and she asked my name, but I wouldn't even hardly look at her. I didn't trust anybody. But she handed me a card with the name of Covenant House on it. The address wasn't far away. I walked and walked and I didn't really know where I was going. I just knew that I didn't want to go back to the group or the street. I couldn't go home. And I found myself outside the door of this Covenant House.

It wasn't like Ben said. No one judged me or looked down on me. They brought me in and treated me like a real person. I showered, was given some clean clothes, some food. I was really hungry. I slept warm and safe for the first time in weeks. I just slept and slept.

That was a couple of months ago. In the time since coming to Covenant House, I've had lots of help from people who care—help looking at my life, what I want to do. I'm going back to school. I've never gone back to the streets. When I'm a bit older, I want to help out by going out, like Carole did the night Mike got beat up, and letting other kids who are stuck on the street know about Covenant House. I want them to know that they have somewhere to go, that there are people who will care about them, who will respect them, who won't judge them, who will just give them help to make the choices that will get them off the street and into a life.

Covenant House—Toronto

Covenant House in Toronto opened its doors in February 1982 in response to increasing numbers of runaway and homeless youths. Since that time, they have had more than 35,000 visits from young people seeking various kinds of help, people who come from all across Canada from many different backgrounds.

The staff at Covenant House are committed to offering immediate help to provide for such basic human needs as food, clothing, showers, medical attention, and safe beds. They offer sanctuary from the dangers of the street and teach skills that are alternatives to the destructive patterns of street life. They provide the structure and stability that allow a young person to develop more long-term goals, and they encourage and counsel these youths in making wise choices to create the kind of life they want to live in the future.

Covenant House is available to help twenty-four hours a day, seven days a week, and is committed to helping young people no matter what kinds of needs they have, no matter what their pasts are or in what conditions they currently find themselves. In addition to having doors open for assistance and comfort, Covenant House provides an outreach program through which trained volunteers go out into the streets and make contact with young people, letting them know that there is a place of safety where they can go if they choose.

2. I am Miguel. With my younger sister and brother, Margarita and Carlos, I live now in Miacatlán, Mexico, where I am part of a huge family of brothers and sisters—more than I can count. We came to live here when I was seven, two years ago. Margarita and

Carlos are just four and six now, and they hardly remember anything before coming here.

But some things I remember. We had a little home in a small village in the mountains. One day soldiers came—my mother and father rushed us all inside the house and told us to hide under the bed. I was so scared. We huddled together while guns were firing, and there was screaming and moaning. And then silence. Still we didn't come out. When we finally did, everybody was dead. Mama, Papa, our Aunt Rosita—everyone. Little Carlos was crying and Margarita was just staring and staring.

The next day some people came. We were hiding again, but finally we came out. We were very hungry and very afraid. They took us in jeeps down the mountain. After that, I don't remember much before coming here.

There's lots of kids like us here. Nobody has parents who are alive, or if they are, no one knows where they are. Margarita didn't talk for a long time. Carlos had bad dreams and would wake up screaming for many weeks. But now they smile all the time. And Margarita—well, you can hardly get her to stop talking now.

This place is called Nuestros Pequeños Hermanos and in English they say it is "Our Little Brothers and Sisters." Everyone here feels like they belong. We go to school, we work in the gardens, we feed the chickens, we wash the dishes. There are other places like this in Mexico, and also in Haiti, Honduras, and Nicaragua. Father Wasson is the priest who started it all, a long time ago. He is our friend and like a father to our family of hundreds. We learn to care for one another and we know that this will always be our home and our family.

Even when I grow up, and after I give a year or more of work and service in return for all I have received, I will still come back to visit and work. I know that because I see so many others who do. They come back, because we are all one family. Margarita and Carlos and I—we belong here now.

Friends of Our Little Brothers and Sisters—Latin America

Friends of Our Little Brothers and Sisters began in Cuernavaca, Mexico, with one child, an orphaned boy who had stolen money from the poor box of the church to buy some food. Father Wasson, a priest, asked police if he might have custody of the child. He was granted custody, and the police also delivered eight more tattered orphans to Father Wasson in the following week. Through the years, more people joined to help, as more and more orphans were given a home. Now there are more than 1,500 orphaned and abandoned children in Mexico, Honduras, and Haiti who receive food, shelter, clothing, education, security, and love in this very large home.

Brothers and sisters in a family are kept together as part of this larger family. All children have the security of knowing they will never be asked to leave. Everyone has a place in the community, with responsibilities for sharing, for work, and for studies. More than 15,000 orphaned and abandoned children have been raised in Our Little Brothers and Sisters since it began.

3. My name is Rob. I grew up in this neighborhood in Philadelphia, and for the first fifteen years of my life, I didn't see much worth really caring about. This is a poor area—lots of people have no work. There's lots of drugs and booze. You get what you can get.

When I got old enough, it didn't take long to get in with the gang. We were the Clymer Street gang then. And anyone who came on our turf from another gang was in for trouble. Or we went looking for it when it didn't come to us.

The gang was like my family. I started to feel like I belonged to it, and I was loyal to everyone in it. There was no way I'd turn on them or betray my brothers—that was the code.

Falaka and David—they understood that. Somehow they knew, and they somehow got all of us to come and live with them. Can you believe it? So all of us moved into their home, and they made us start to care about our lives more. They told us about *Umoja*—it's a Swahili word that means "unity"—and about things like peace, self-respect, caring for one another, caring for ourselves.

And then guys from other gangs started to turn up on the doorstep. We weren't enemies anymore. Everybody who wanted in, and who was willing to let go of the old ways of the gang, was welcome. More and more of them came, and the family kept growing.

We've got a whole block of houses on this street now. There's another way to live than the way of the gang. Falaka and David showed me that. They showed me that they loved me, and they were willing to work to make my life better and teach me how to love others, how to love myself, how to care enough to demand it from myself to make a better life. We all still help one another now—all of us from the old gang. But it doesn't stop with just us. It keeps on going.

House of Umoja—Boystown

It was 1969 when Falaka and David Fattah learned that their sixteen-year-old son, Robin, was deeply involved with the Clymer Street gang in Philadelphia. They were shocked and terrified for their son's life. Searching for a way to help, Falaka felt confused and angry, and wondered what made these young people choose to be part of the street gang. David knew that many of them saw the gang as a kind of family. Being without a real family themselves, they needed something they could feel they belonged to.

Falaka was inspired to take action. If family was what these youths needed, family was what she would give them. Soon fifteen members of the gang were invited to move into the Fattah's four-room house, and they did. Frightened young people from other gangs started turning up soon after. No one was turned away. David and Falaka had learned about Umoja; it is a Swahili family system rooted in self-discipline. It strives for peace, love, and justice in the world. They put the ideals of Umoja into practice and taught these ideals to those who came to live with them.

In their home, which has now grown to twenty-four houses on one street, the Fattahs give trust and respect to young boys who are convicted in the juvenile courts. With David and Falaka, these young people are treated firmly, but everyone understands that they are loved and cared for, which is what makes it work, like a family works.

4. My name is Ahmed. I live now in a little village, in a home, in a forest in Africa, in a little country called *Rwanda*. I have a mother and brothers and sisters, but I wasn't born with them.

   Once I lived in another village. It was by the river. All my other family was there, and we had cattle and some chickens, and we had land where we grew vegetables. We were happy, my mother, aunts, uncles, grandmother, grandfather. My father worked a long way away in the town. He came home when he could and he would bring us food from town. Then we would have a big celebration.

It seemed like there were always the ones who lived across the river. "One day they will come," my mother often told me, "and when they do, you must run and not look back." Sometimes people disappeared, and I never went to the river alone.

One day we saw them coming, and I ran away, into the forest. I ran and ran. It got dark and I climbed a tree, curled up into a branch, and sort of slept. Somehow I knew. The last thing I heard my mother say was, "Ahmed, keep running," and the next day I just kept on going, getting as far as I could from the river and the danger from those who had crossed it to our village.

I got hungry and tired and scared. I came at last to a road and there were others too who were running, trying to get away. I met someone from our village. He told me everyone had been killed.

I went numb then. I just kept walking. Lots of other people were walking, too. I didn't feel anything anymore. I wasn't hungry or thirsty.

We came to a town and some people gave us food. I didn't eat. A woman and a man asked me questions. I don't think I talked. They took me with them and brought me here to this village. It is a long way from my other home. There's a lot I don't remember.

It took me a long time not to be numb. Many of the others who live here have had things like this happen. We have lost our homes and families. But we have found new ones. This is named the SOS Children's Village. There are several homes, each with six or seven children, each with a mother. I miss my first home village. All of us who remember have these feelings. But I am very grateful to have been given a new home. Here, too, I am cared for and I also am able to go to school. I will never forget my mother, my first family, my first home. None of us will. Still we are glad we have one another and that there are people who love us, who feed us, comfort us, and protect us.

SOS Children's Villages—Worldwide

Hermann Gmeiner founded the SOS Children's Villages just after World War II, moved by the plight of the many homeless and orphaned children left after the destruction and upheaval in Europe. Since that time, the villages have spread throughout the world, with 325 of them in more than 125 countries. These villages give a home, a place of belonging, to more than 180,000 children.

Knowing that children need the love and security of a family, Hermann Gmeiner established a collection of several homes clustered together to create a small village. Every home has a mother who lives with and cares for the children as if they were her own children. These homes build a sense of belonging, security, trust, and family, important features in the healthy growth of children.

Evaluation for "In Another's Shoes"

Name: _____ Date: _____

1. The character is appropriate for the story. The name of the character and the place where he or she lives is described. The events fit the part of the world where the story takes place. .... /10

2. The story has a beginning, a middle, and an end. The events are logically connected. The story details are developed to make it interesting and realistic. .... /20

3. The story describes the situation that shows how the person's rights were not respected. It tells how the person got help and from where the help came. It tells the feelings of the person both before and after getting help............. /20

4. Punctuation, capitals, and spelling are according to standard usage. Sentence structure is correct. Final copy is double-spaced, hand-written or typed on one side of the paper, with title, name of author, and date. .... /20

   TOTAL .... /70

We All Belong Here

Preceding activities prepared students to realize that there are many places and situations in the world where basic rights of children and other living things are not being met. Students have also considered that there are people actively working to change this predicament.

This activity gives students an opportunity to express these ideas in song and to discuss their understandings.

▶ Structure

class, small groups, or individuals

▶ Material

1 copy of song or lyrics of song for each student

▶ Time

1 class period

▶ Procedure

Step 1: Distribute the lyrics for "We Belong Here—All of Us" to each student or to small groups.

Step 2: Ask students to read the lyrics and write responses to the following questions as a class, a small group, or an individual:

What thoughts, feelings, or images come to mind when you read the words?

What are you reminded of, or what associations do the words bring to mind?

What ideas or situations could have been behind writing such a song? What other way could these ideas or situations be communicated or expressed?

We Belong Here - All Of Us

words and music by Alanda Greene

We Belong Here—All of Us

We can take a picture of our planet from afar—
See it floating there in space.
Looking from that distance it's easier to see
That the world is home to the whole human race.
We all share the heavens; we share the stars.
We share the wind and clouds and trees.
And so the bounty that the earth is bringing forth
Could be shared throughout our home more evenly.

Chorus:
For we belong here, all of us,
Beneath the sky's blue dome.
The sun gives light to everyone.
This is everybody's home.

In so many places all over this world
There are children who have need.
People with no shelter, no water fit to drink,
No medicine, no food,
But still mouths to feed.
Yet there is abundance in places of the earth,
Not just in goods but also care.
As minds and hearts awake to those who are without
This bounty we will find a way to share.

Chorus

Choosing the Future

This activity encourages children to have a positive image of the future. Often, when asked to give a description of their imagined world of tomorrow, children present bleak visions of destruction. They sometimes joke with a dark humor about such things as the extensive pollution to come, so much "that a skunk smell will be like perfume," or how insects "will glow in the dark from having so much radiation." It is important that children hold an optimistic potential in their imaginations, the idea that there is hope and that the effort needed to actualize this positive vision is worth it.

▶ **Structure**

    class, small group, individual

▶ **Material**

    imagination

    1 copy of lyrics "Choosing the Future"

▶ **Time**

    1 or 2 class periods *(30 to 40 minutes)*

▶ **Procedure**

    Step 1: Ask students to sit or lie down in comfortable positions where they are not touching anyone else. Encourage them to find positions in which they can fully relax. If you have enough space for them to lie comfortably on their backs, this pose is the best for relaxation, but the method you use may depend on the culture of your students. Sitting at desks or tables with heads down works well also. Assess your group and aim for the situation that gives the most quiet.

Step 2: Read aloud the instructions for progressive relaxation in a calm, clear voice. Read them slowly in a gentle, relaxing tone. Move progressively through the body with a tense-relax process, until every student has progressively relaxed every body part. Pause between each set of instructions to allow students to relax that part completely. This process helps children focus inward and connect with their imaginations.

Relaxation Process

Close your eyes. Pay attention to your breathing. Let your breath flow deeply, quietly, and slowly, into and out of your body, gently pushing your abdomen in and out as it does so.

Count to four slowly as you breathe in. One, two, three, four. And the same as you breathe out. One, two, three, four. Repeat the breaths, keeping the same rhythm for the intake and release of your breath. Do not force or strain, but let this process be relaxed and even. Keep this even, rhythmic, slow counting going silently with your breath as you do the following.

Tense the muscles in your feet, tight and tighter. Then release. Feel the relaxation as it enters your feet.

Now tense the muscles in your legs, tight and tighter. Then release. Feel your legs relax.

Now tense your abdomen and buttocks. Tight and tighter. Release, and feel the relaxation as it comes through your body. You are completely relaxed from the waist down.

Now tense your hands and arms, as tightly as possible. Tight. Then release. Feel your hands and arms relax.

Tense your chest, shoulders, and back. Tight and tighter. Now release. Feel your chest, shoulders, and back as they completely relax.

Now tighten your neck and jaw. Tight and tighter. Then release. Feel as your neck and jaw relax.

Now tense your face. Push everything toward the center of your face. And relax. Feel the relaxation spread over your face, your eyes, your ears, your lips and tongue, your nose and teeth, your scalp and all your hair.

Everything is relaxed now, but your mind is alert. Picture and feel yourself floating on a white cloud, high in the blue sky, a cool breeze on your face, warmth from the sun on your chest.

In your mind, imagine that this cloud gently carries you to the future. You softly float to the world a hundred years in the future. You look around and see this world.

Then you relax again on your cloud as it carries you gently back to the present.

I will count backward from five and you will slowly sit up and share, if you wish, what you experienced in the future world. Five, four, three, two, one.

Step 3: Invite students to share the world they envisioned. If a majority seem to have negative images, ask students to relax again. Guide them into a receptive state again, using as much of the relaxation as needed. Bring them to the stage of arriving on the world of the future. Then guide the vision to help students create a positive picture:

See a world that is lush and alive. Green grass waves in the sunlight. The air smells crisp and fresh, like a spring morning. Flowers grow in many colors through the grass. Birds are flying in the blue sky overhead, chirping happy calls. The trees bordering the field are lush and green. Think of other things you see in this world. Think about what the people are doing. Think about what the animals are doing.

In the same manner as you did earlier, bring the students back to the present and explain the importance of holding a positive vision for the future.

Step 4: Distribute copies of the lyrics for "Choosing the Future" to each student. If you have music accompaniment, introduce the song by singing it together, inviting students to join in singing as soon as they grasp the melody. The words suggest ways to meet needs of people in the world who are not having their basic rights respected.

Step 5: Read the following information to students.

Thousands of children die every day from diseases caused by unclean drinking water. Cheap and simple medicine could prevent their deaths, yet they have no access to it. Neither have they access to clean water.

Thousands of children starve to death daily and thousands more are hungry and malnourished.

Thousands have no opportunity for education and will never learn to read or write, and therefore never have the opportunity to develop their ability to get out of the poverty cycle.

At the same time, the annual world expenditure on armaments is nearly a trillion dollars.

Many say that humankind owes the child the best it has to give. Is this debt being paid? Are we giving the best to the children of the world?

Step 6: Invite students to comment on the passage and encourage diversity in their responses. The armaments spending may not be an easy issue to resolve. What is important is that students consider it thoughtfully and caringly.

Step 7: Gives students time to read the lyrics carefully. Ask students to get in small groups and come up with additional sentences that begin with: "How about a world . . . ?" Have them record the sentences and share them with the class.

Step 8: Instruct students to copy and complete the following statements in their reflective journals:

The best thing about my imagined world of the future is . . .

Something I can do to help bring about that world is . . .

Choosing the Future

words and music by Alanda Greene

How a-bout a world where the air___ is all___ clean, where
How a-bout a world where the peo-ple work to - ge - ther, and
How a-bout a world where there's no one who goes hun-gry but

dir - ty things are guns and shells and war? How a-bout a world where there's
all the ar-mies join to work for peace? How a-bout a world where the
all the mis-sile fac-t'ries are shut down? How a-bout a world where all

wa - ter for us all, but nu - clear bombs aren't built a - ny - more?
wealth is shared by all and it's the wea - pons spending that will cease?
chil - dren dream in peace and think - ing of the future brings no frown?

Chorus

Will I be part of the prob - lem or part of the cure? What

choi - ces will I make with my hu - man - i - ty? Will I be

part of the prob-lem or part of the cure? What will I choose to be?

Choosing the Future

How about a world where the air is all clean,
Where dirty things are guns and shells and war?
How about a world where there's water for us all,
But nuclear bombs aren't built anymore?

Chorus:
Will I be part of the problem or part of the cure?
What choices will I make with my humanity?
Will I be part of the problem or part of the cure?
What will I choose to be?

How about a world where the people work together
And all the armies join to work for peace?
How about a world where the wealth is shared by all,
And it's the weapons' spending that will cease?

Chorus

How about a world where there's no one who goes hungry,
And all the missile factories are shut down?
How about a world where all children dream in peace
And thinking of the future brings no frown?

Chorus

Envisioning the Future

D rawing or painting an image of the world of the future is an effective way to encourage students to hold a positive vision. Thoughts and feelings represented through various methods of symbolic expression—image, word, gesture—are strengthened, are given power to be an active force with the individual. So many influences contribute to building negative expectations that it is important to counter them as effectively as possible.

▶ **Material**

> paper
>
> pencils
>
> crayons
>
> paints

▶ **Time**

> 1 or 2 class periods

▶ **Procedure**

> **Step 1:** Ask students to recall the scenes, images, pictures, and colors of the positive world they envisioned during the second relaxation in activity 14. Have them individually choose from their mental pictures one that would make an effective visual representation of the ideas, thoughts, and feelings they experienced. They can have several images combined or one picture or scene.

Step 2: Have students create their vision using the materials provided.

Step 3: Display all the work and ask students to tell individually what they chose for their pictures and why.

Step 4: Have students complete the following thoughts in their reflective journals:

The drawing or painting of my world of the future shows my thoughts, ideas, and feelings in this way:

What I like best about this piece of art is . . .

What I would like to improve if I did it again is . . .

Interviews
from the Future

This activity builds on what students have learned and experienced in the previous two activities, further strengthening a positive view of the future.

▶ **Structure**

> pairs or triads (*1 person is the press; 1 or 2 others are residents of a future time being interviewed*)

▶ **Time**

> 1 or 2 class periods

▶ **Procedure**

> **Step 1:** Ask students to imagine that they are old residents of the world a hundred years in the future, in the positively envisioned world they represented in their art. Ask them to imagine that they were told stories, handed down through generations, about the very dangerous time in Earth's history near the close of the twentieth century. Because they know this information, a reporter who is compiling a history of this time is interviewing them. The reporter wants to focus on how Earth emerged as the place of beauty and harmony it is now. What events took place? What did people do?

> **Step 2:** Ask students to discuss these questions and to present such an interview.

Step 3: Ask students to record and complete responses to the following phrases in their reflective journals:

The most effective interview was _____
_____because . . .

The most effective aspect of my interview was . . .

Something I heard that really made me think was . . .

Who Gives a Hoot? Forests and the Spotted Owl

This activity acquaints students with the issue concerning the spotted owl and the logging of old growth forests. Students examine information about these owls and their habitat to decide which people would most likely hold which points of view. The activity helps students become familiar with various arguments. Afterward, students take on various roles to consider the situation from the perspective of various interest groups, learning that there is more than one way to view a problem.

▶ **Structure**

class, small group, individuals

▶ **Material**

copied and cut list of statements concerning the spotted owl controversy

tape or tacks

▶ **Time**

1 class period

▶ **Procedure**

Step 1: Read the background information about the spotted owl controversy to the class. If necessary, read it twice, so that students have a strong sense of the issues involved. You may want to assign the Forest Talk crossword puzzle for students to complete in pairs or small groups; it encourages familiarity with terms that students may not have often encountered previously.

Step 2: Divide the class into small groups. Copy the list of statements and information concerning the spotted owl. Cut the statements into separate pieces and divide them evenly among the groups.

Step 3: Put the following titles side by side on the chalkboard or the bulletin board: "Environmental Concerns," "Timber Companies Concerns," and "Concerns of Both or Neither."

Step 4: Ask students to read the statements you gave them earlier and decide among themselves under which heading that particular statement would best fit.

Step 5: In turn, reporters from each group tape or pin these statements under the headings they deem appropriate. Each reporter reads each statement aloud to the class as it is placed. Students from other groups can challenge the chosen placement for a given statement and suggest another heading where they think it would be better placed, supporting their opinion. Students from any group may also ask for clarification as to why a particular statement was placed where it was.

Background

The spotted owl is a chocolate brown bird with white patches on its feathers, which give the appearance of spots that inspired its name. These owls are shy birds, rarely seen. They live in the old growth forests of the Pacific Northwest. Each bird has only one mate, and pairs make their nests in the thick moss on branches of ancient trees. A single pair of spotted owls requires an area of forest ranging from 1,000 acres in the warmer areas of the south to 4,000 acres farther north. The owl's main source of food is the flying squirrel, which also inhabits these old forests. Although spotted owls are sometimes seen in younger forests, they do not seem to breed there.

The old growth forests also produce the most valuable timber. In the 1980s, old growth forests were the source of 30 percent of the lumber produced in the United States. In recent years they have been extensively logged. Where once the old growth forests covered more than 17 million acres in the United States, now no more than 7 million acres remain, and some estimates say that the area that remains is closer to 3 million acres.

With the reduction of old growth forests due to logging, certain kinds of wildlife, such as spotted owls, have been decreasing in number. Their habitat is disappearing. In 1986 the Audubon Society issued a report saying that the number of spotted owls had decreased so much that they were in danger of extinction. As a result of this report, the owls were declared a threatened species under the Endangered Species Act. In Canada, where fewer than a hundred pairs of owls are believed to exist, they have been put on the Endangered Species List, which means their survival is considered at great risk.

This listing has restricted large areas of old growth forest from logging in order to preserve a habitat for the spotted owls. Timber companies and loggers are outraged, saying that this little bird has caused loss of money and loss of jobs. In the years that have followed this protection, many timber companies have undertaken studies and claim that the spotted owl is not as threatened as was believed and that there are more pairs of them than previously thought. Some people have maintained that maybe the spotted owl will have to become extinct, that the cost of keeping it alive by keeping such a large area of old growth forest protected is too high. A popular bumper sticker in the United States said "Save a Logger, Kill an Owl," while in Canada, the head of the International Woodworkers commented to loggers, "If you see a spotted owl, kill it."

Others claim that the preservation of these forests is itself important, not just for the spotted owl but for the varied species that live in these forests and nowhere else. These people maintain also that someone has to speak for the rights of these birds to live and of the forests they inhabit to live also.

The debate on this issue continues.

Statements about the Issue

The jobs that are lost because of environmental protection aren't really lost. They become different jobs. For example, one study estimated that environmental protection in the United States in 1992 cost 3 million jobs but created 4 million jobs.

Logging might destroy the larger and most beautiful trees, but one forest researcher's study suggests that it actually increases the biodiversity of the forest by increasing the number of species that can live in it. As sunlight is able to reach the forest floor, more kinds of plants can then live there.

Between 1980 and 1988, lumber production in the United States increased by 20 percent in the Northwest. Yet 14,000 jobs in that industry were lost, mainly because of using more modern equipment. It isn't environmental protection causing loss of jobs; it's technology.

The national forests belong to all the people, not just the logging companies. They belong to the plants and animals that depend on them. Humans don't have a right to log them all.

Limiting the logging in the Pacific Northwest may preserve the old growth forest there, but it just means that the logging will occur other places in the world, such as Brazil or Malaysia. The limit doesn't really protect the forests of the world; it just means the United States and Canada logging jobs and income from logging.

The national forests were established to provide a perpetual supply of timber, not to be an unlimited wildlife sanctuary.

Old growth forests have long-term benefits and importance. The issue isn't just about preserving the spotted owl, but about a whole ecosystem. It may be that these ancient forests play an important role that hasn't been discovered yet. They need to be preserved. Logging the old growth forests means that plants and animals that can only live in these areas do not survive.

Nature has its own logging practices in the form of forest fires, tornadoes, and insect infestation. Nature takes down big trees and replaces them with young saplings, the same way the timber companies do.

Clear cutting is what endangers the spotted owl. If select logging and shelter cuts of small areas are the kind of logging practices used, the owl can survive.

The number of spotted owls is declining every year.

The jobs in the forest are short lived. When the remaining old growth is cut down in a few years, there will be none left to log anyway, so why not just stop it earlier and save some of these forests? The long-term importance of the forest is worth more than short-term jobs.

A single bird takes up too much land.

The economy of this region is based on forestry and is dependent on it. People have to count somewhere.

We don't have to shut down the whole forest industry to protect the spotted owl, but we have to have a plan that makes sure this species isn't forced into extinction.

Studies conducted in 1992 in Oregon and Colorado show that spotted owl populations are decreasing by 10 percent per year and that female owls are not being replaced.

Preventing logging in old growth forest is a misguided attempt to conserve this endangered species.

Spotted owl pairs need such a large area for just one pair that there were probably never very many of them. Maybe they aren't really decreasing in number.

It was estimated in 1992 that logging the national forests costs more money than was earned in timber sales, because of the high cost of administering the logging programs in these areas. Tax payers are paying to have the forests cut down.

What's more important—that a person has a job or some bird is allowed to live?

The spotted owls that live in the younger forests have been forced to go there by logging of the old growth forests and probably won't survive.

Creatures have the ability to adjust to new conditions because the environmental conditions are always changing. The spotted owl will learn to live somewhere else.

The rights of people to work have to be considered in this somewhere.

Spotted owls that live in California outside of the national forest are able to live there because there is still a remnant of the old growth forest and the area has never been clear cut. When these remnants are gone, the owls will be gone, too.

A 1991 report from the United States Department of Fish and Wildlife said that all data show that spotted owls reproduced only in old growth forest, even if occasionally they were seen elsewhere.

Trees grow back. The trees cut down now for logging will grow back in fifty to a hundred years. Many logged areas are replanted and the forest will return after it is logged.

In 1992 a study of forests that were clear cut about fifty to ninety years ago showed that they were not the old growth forests that they had once been. They were missing many of the plants that are located in an old growth forest. They look the same, but they aren't the same.

Studies done in recent years suggest that spotted owls are more numerous and widespread than earlier thought. They aren't so dependent on the old growth forest as was thought.

Crossword Puzzle: Forest Talk

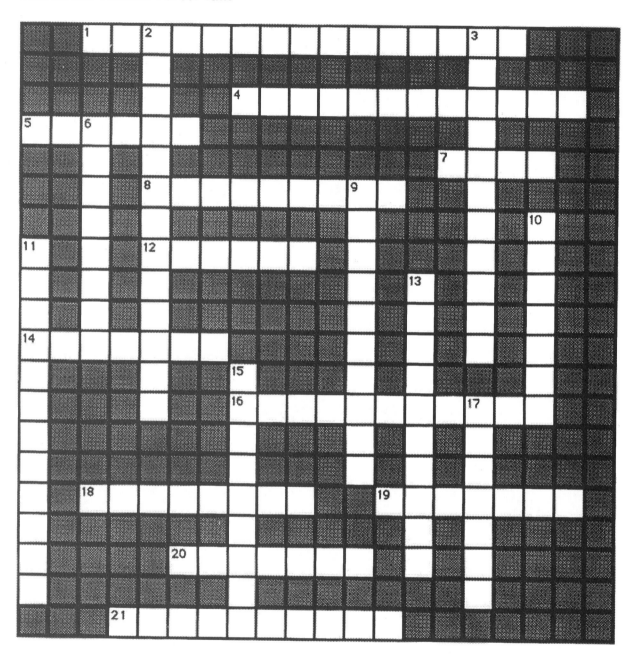

Across

1. Ancient regions of trees that have not been logged
4. A wide range of living things in an area
5. Bird of prey
7. Collected information
8. Interdependent cyclic relationship of living things in a region
12. Logs taken from a forest to sell
14. A name for a group of one kind of living thing
16. The surroundings
18. A way of logging that takes all the logs from an area of forest
19. An evergreen tree that has cones
20. To grow less in size or number
21. Rare, shy raptor that lives in old growth forests

Down

2. The disappearance of forest regions on Earth
3. A way of living that does not deplete Earth's ecosystems
6. To save or protect
9. Threatened with extinction
10. The area in which something lives
11. The practice of keeping things from being destroyed
13. Using tools and machines to do work
15. A logging method that takes only some trees from an area
17. Something that did exist and no longer does

Word List: Forest Talk
Choose your answers from the following list.

Biodiversity	Ecosystem	Raptor
Clear cut	Endangered	Select cut
Conifer	Environment	Species
Conservation	Extinct	Spotted owl
Data	Habitat	Sustainable
Decline	Old growth forest	Technology
Deforestation	Preserve	Timber

Solution to Forest Talk

Who Gives a Hoot?
Changing Perspectives

After participating in the previous activity, students have some sense of the background concerning the spotted owl and the logging of the old growth forests in the Pacific Northwest. Students have also been exposed to a range of statements about how this issue should be resolved.

In this activity, students have the opportunity to consider the issue from the perspective of a logger who wants to cut the timber in the old growth forest, from the perspective of a spotted owl able to voice a position, and from the perspective of a government official who is hearing the views put forth by the former positions.

▶ **Structure**

groups of 3

▶ **Time**

1 class period

▶ **Procedure**

Step 1:   Divide the class into groups of three. Begin with each person taking a role: one person speaks as if having the voice of a spotted owl; one person speaks as a logger who needs the timber for continued employment; the third person is a government official who listens to the other two as they take turns presenting their view. Basically, the first two want to present evidence that will convince the government official to decide in their favor.

Step 2:   After five minutes (or a bit more, depending on students' verbal fluency), everyone takes a role different from the first one. That is, the logger becomes the government official, the owl becomes the logger, and the government official becomes the owl. Repeat the process.

Step 3:   After approximately five minutes, change again so that each person again speaks from a new view.

Step 4:   Regroup the class and discuss the following:

What feelings did you experience?

What did you notice after speaking from a point of view different from the one you began with?

What changes in your understanding did you experience after taking all three roles?

In what ways, if any, can the rights of the forest, the spotted owls, and the loggers all be respected?

What solutions can you suggest to this problem?

Step 5: Working individually, students copy the following phrases and complete them in their personal journals:

The view I found most difficult to support was . . .

A change in opinion or understanding I experienced was . . .

Evaluation Record

Activity:
Who Gives a Hoot? Forests and the Spotted Owl

Name: _____ Date: _____

Identifying the Likely Source of a Statement—Small Group Work:

Focused on task, avoided
distractions or disruptions ..../5

Contributed ideas ..../5

Listened to others ..../5

Taking a Role and Changing Position

Thoughtful presentation of
current position ..../5

Able to shift view and speak
from a different position ..../5

Maintained the current voice or role ..../5

Whole Group Discussion

Contributed by asking questions
or listening attentively to the
comments or questions of others ..../10

A Gathering of Beings

In this activity, students adopt the identity of a being from the mineral, animal, or plant kingdom, and through relaxation and imagination, experience the world from the perspective of that being. The preceding activity, which allowed students to speak from the point of view of the spotted owl, has prepared students to carry the process of seeing from another perspective one step further.

▶ Structure

class, individuals, pairs

▶ Time

1 class period

▶ Procedure

Step 1: Choose a method of giving an identity to each student. The most direct way is to ask students to select an animal, plant, or mineral. The drawback with using this approach is that an even representation of kingdoms doesn't usually occur. Somehow being an eagle or a grizzly bear carries more appeal than being prairie grass or a river.

A good way to assign a more balanced representation of identities and still give students some personal choice is to use a page with three rectangles marked *A*, *P*, and *M* (animal, plant, and mineral). Make enough copies of this page to allow one card per student when the rectangles are cut apart. Cut apart the cards, mix them, and randomly distribute them, one per student. If a student gets an *M* card, then possible choices include mountain, river, ocean, wind, or soil. A *P* offers the plant kingdom, from sequoia pines to ocean algae. And, of course, the *A* cards allows students to choose from the animal kingdom, with the exclusion of humans.

A third way to assign identities is to liken the process to a random genetic code assignment—you take whatever identity you find yourself given, just as we did in finding ourselves human. In this case, copy pages with the names of various beings from plant, animal, and mineral kingdoms written in the rectangles. Cut these out, shuffle them, and randomly distribute them, one per student.

Step 2: After each student has an identity, conduct the relaxation exercise. (Review the procedure in activity 14.)

Step 3: After students have completed the relaxation exercise, ask them to imagine that they are ambassadors, or representatives, for the species they have been assigned or have chosen. They are gathered together in a kind of United Nations assembly, which could be called a "United Beings Assembly," to circulate and speak to ambassadors of other nations or realms. Depending on your students, you may have to explain the concept of ambassadors: representatives of countries living in different countries, speaking and acting on behalf of their own countries.

Step 4: Ask students to gather in groups of three or four and to introduce themselves to one another. Students take turns speaking to the others, telling about the kind of life they represent, and what they have observed on Earth in their particular habitat or sphere of existence. For example, the wind might speak of how the smoke from factories and car exhaust fumes have caused it to discolor, allowed it to carry harmful substances to other areas, and caused difficulty with seeing or breathing in large cities. It may speak of times when it carried refreshing coolness and moist, clean air from over the ocean. It may speak of feeling sad that it can no longer work in this way. It may speak of the joy it feels when people build windmills to allow the wind to help produce a nonpolluting source of energy.

Step 5: After a few minutes, give students a signal to change groups. Have them change enough so that they talk with almost all of the other students in the class.

Step 6: Gather everyone in a circle. Ask students to imagine that a person is in the center of the circle, an ambassador from the human species. Invite students to speak to the human from their perspectives as other beings. What would they like to say to the human? What would be important for the human to realize and understand about the various other beings that live on Earth?

Step 7: Working individually, have students copy and complete the following phrases in their reflective journals:

The most notable aspect of my imagined existence as a _____ was . . .

Some insights, thoughts, or understandings I experienced in this activity were . . .

The strongest feeling I experienced was . . .

A Gathering of Beings: Relaxation and Imagination Exercise

Tell students that they will be participating in another relaxation exercise. This time they will be asked to experience looking at the world from a perspective other than human. When you reach the point in the relaxation when they are looking through another's eyes, students should imagine that they are the kind of being they have either chosen or been assigned.

Read the relaxation process on pages 76–77, including the paragraph, "Everything is relaxed now, but the mind is alert. Picture and feel yourself floating on a white cloud, high in the blue sky, a cool breeze on your face, warmth from the sun on your chest."

From that point, continue reading the following paragraphs, pausing substantially after any questions to allow students time for silent, inner exploration.

Feel yourself totally relaxed and peaceful and floating on this cloud. You are gently carried along on a breeze, and gradually feel yourself being set down on Earth again. As you mentally open your eyes and look at the world around you, you realize that you have become another kind of being. You are no longer a human. You have another kind of existence.

Look around at the world. What do you see? How does the world look different to you when you view it with your new way of seeing?

What appears beautiful to you as you gaze on the world? What is not beautiful?

What sounds do you hear in your world? Where do they come from? Which sounds seem pleasing to you? Which sounds do you find offensive and disturbing?

What smells, what scents do you notice? Focus on them. Are they pleasing or unpleasant smells? Where do they come from?

You return to your white cloud, sit upon it again, feel yourself gently lifted above the ground, and your cloud drifts over Earth, giving you a good view of it. You see all that is happening to Earth from your perspective as another form of being. What things do you see?

What do you feel as you look upon the world?

Feel yourself gently set to Earth again, where you quietly think over all that you have experienced through perceiving Earth as another form of being.

Encourage students to maintain their imaginary identities as you give them the instructions for being ambassadors described earlier in the activity and for communicating with the imagined human.

A Gathering of Beings

A	P	M
A	P	M
A	P	M
A	P	M
A	P	M

Spider	Ant	Earthworm
Wind	Pond	Pine tree
Wild Rose	Bluebell	Tortoise
Antelope	Grizzly bear	Fir tree
Prairie grass	Blackbird	Caribou

A Gathering of Beings

Mountain	**Eagle**	**Swallow**
River	**Otter**	**Deer**
Ocean	**Whale**	**Wolf**
Salmon	**Dolphin**	**Cougar**
Woodpecker	**Marten**	**Fieldmouse**

Who Speaks for Earth?

Students will have discussed various environmental problems in the preceding activities. Imagining these problems from the perspective of other life forms promotes understanding as to the impacts they have on Earth. Students have done many activities to become acquainted with rights and responsibilities regarding children. With this previous learning, they have the background that enables a thoughtful consideration of such questions as, Who speaks for Earth? What are the rights of plants, animals, and ecosystems? Who gives voice to honor their rights? What responsibilities do humans have to uphold these rights?

▶ Structure

small groups, class, individuals

▶ Material

chart paper

felt markers

tape or pins for posting charts

▶ Time

1 class period

▶ Procedure

Step 1: Review with the class the ten points of the *Declaration of the Rights of the Child.*

Step 2: Have students work in small groups to consider the rights of Earth, and of the plants, animals, and ecosystems that belong to it. What would a *Declaration of the Rights of Earth* contain? Ask them to select a recorder from their group members and to brainstorm as many things as they can, thinking back to the types of beings that participated in the Gathering of Beings activity. It may help to review brainstorming guidelines.

Step 3: After recording as many points as possible, each group deletes, combines, condenses, and revises items until it has ten points. The recorder writes these points on chart paper, and a reporter reads these to the class. After each group reads its ten points aloud, they post the chart where it is visible.

Step 4: As a class, examine all the points posted on the charts. Ask for suggestions for combining, condensing, or revising these points to create one document of ten points, which would be a *Declaration of the Rights of Earth*. Record the suggestions, guiding possibilities where necessary, until the class achieves such a declaration. Post this declaration.

Step 5: Have students return to their small groups and discuss the responsibilities that humans have to uphold these rights for Earth. Ask groups to list as many responsibilities as they can imagine for each right listed in the declaration.

Step 6: Ask each group to offer, one at a time, a responsibility they have chosen. Circulate from one group to the next, with each group offering a responsibility that has not been mentioned, until you have created a class list of responsibilities to post beside the *Declaration of the Rights of Earth*. Title the list of responsibilities *Declaration of Responsibilities to Earth*.

Step 7: Have students work individually to copy and complete the following phrases:

When I think about the rights of Earth and its plants and animals, I feel . . .

When I think about my responsibilities to Earth and its plants and animals, I . . .

Evaluation for Who Speaks for Earth?

Name: _____ Date: _____

After each criterion, mark a line on the continuum that reflects the quality of the student's work.

	Student	Teacher
	weak _____ strong	weak _____ strong
Small Group Work		
contributed ideas	I _____ I	I _____ I
listened to others	I _____ I	I _____ I
avoided distractions	I _____ I	I _____ I
focused on task	I _____ I	I _____ I
spoke considerately	I _____ I	I _____ I
Class Work		
contributed ideas	I _____ I	I _____ I
listened to others	I _____ I	I _____ I
avoided distractions	I _____ I	I _____ I
focused on task	I _____ I	I _____ I
spoke considerately	I _____ I	I _____ I
Personal Journal		
thoughtful response	I _____ I	I _____ I
thorough response	I _____ I	I _____ I
legible, neat writing	I _____ I	I _____ I

Letter Writing

Amnesty International emerged in 1969 from the indignant anger of one man, Peter Benenson, who decided enough was enough when he read about yet another man who had been imprisoned for his political beliefs. Peter was determined to do something about this injustice and felt that if he could let others know and inspire them to take up the pen for this cause, they could influence the government who was wrongfully holding the man in jail. He took out a large ad in a well-known newspaper, where he described the situation and asked people to write letters on behalf of the prisoner. Hundreds of people who read about the situation shared his outrage. They wrote letters in protest, reminding the government of the country who held this man prisoner that such an action violated the *Universal Declaration of Human Rights,* which had been signed by all members of the United Nations. Since one item clearly states that a person cannot be jailed for the nonviolent expression of his or her ideas, the government was not keeping this agreement. The man was released from jail.

This successful campaign led Benenson to found and organize Amnesty International. Today, at any given time, more than 5,000 letter campaigns focus on prisoners of conscience—that is, people imprisoned because of the nonviolent expression of their beliefs. The letters are written by various groups of the worldwide network of amnesty volunteers, who number over a million people. Hundreds of thousands of people have been released as a result of these letters. In addition, many people have stated that during the years spent in prison, the letters written on their behalf gave them hope and courage. Amnesty International accepts as subjects of their letter campaigns only people who have been imprisoned for the nonviolent expression of their beliefs.

Using the *Universal Declaration of Human Rights* as a guide, members of Amnesty International write courteous letters to governments of countries where violations of rights occur. The letters point out that all nations in the UN have signed this document and agreed to uphold these rights. Therefore, it is appropriate to remind the country of the agreement and to request that it respect the agreement by releasing the prisoner. Sometimes the letters ask the government to investigate improper behavior by military or police forces or to investigate disappearances and illegal actions within the country.

This activity requires students to perform a similar task. In the activity called "A Gathering of Beings," students imagined various environmental problems and discussed these as if they were ambassadors from other kingdoms. They expressed their thoughts and feelings to an imagined representative of the human species. Students are prepared now to select a particular environmental problem (such as deforestation; soil, water, or air pollution; disappearance of plant and animal species; or ozone depletion) and understand it as a possible violation under the class's *Declaration of the Rights of Earth.*

Students are asked to write individual, courteous letters that identify the specific rights being violated, describe the situations causing the violations, and request that the violations cease. Emphasize that the letter is to be written in a polite manner. Such letter writing gives students practice in focusing on the facts of a situation rather than on the emotion, and in expressing these facts clearly. Name calling or blaming in anger only causes people to be defensive and unlikely to consider requests. Let students know that they may well feel very angry but that courteous language achieves results.

Each student decides where his or her letter would appropriately be sent, whether to a national, state (or provincial), or regional government; to a company or organization; to a certain group of people; or even to a certain way of thinking or behaving. Finally, the student includes a statement of personal commitment in the letter, writing what he or she intends to do to contribute to this right being honored.

▶ Structure

individuals

▶ Material

posted *Declaration of the Rights of Earth*

1 copy for each student of letter-writing guide sheets

1 copy for each student of evaluation criteria

▶ Time

1 or more class periods, depending on the amount of work students do outside of class and on your students' writing ability

▶ Procedure

Step 1: Read the description at the beginning of this activity, or describe to the class the work of Amnesty International—how it began and how it works now.

Step 2: Ask students to consider various environmental problems that they know about or have thought about in the preceding activities. Ask them to look at the *Declaration of the Rights of Earth*, which they have created and posted, to see if there is a right listed that is connected to the environmental problem.

Step 3: When a student recognizes a relationship between one or more rights and a particular issue, he or she composes a letter in the manner that Amnesty International encourages, which means a courteous letter stating the facts, pointing out how the rights are being violated, and requesting that the violation cease. Students will write these letters on behalf of members of Earth in the plant, animal, or mineral kingdoms.

Step 4: Explain to students that letters from Amnesty International are usually sent to the heads of governments. For this variation, students will have to determine to whom their letters are to be addressed. They may be addressing their thoughts to a whole group who use wasteful packaging in the products they buy, or to people who use sprays and styrofoam that release CFCs (chlorofluorocarbons) and contribute to the breakdown of the ozone layer. They may wish to write to a local government to require stricter laws concerning polluting the local streams.

Reading the following examples may be helpful.

If you are aware of a specific company who is known to be polluting, you may choose to write a courteous letter to that company and maybe even send it. You may also address your words to all the people who buy products from that company and encourage them not to do so until the pollution is decreased. If the issue is pollution of the air through car exhaust fumes, you may want to write a letter to all people who choose to drive a car when another, nonpolluting or less polluting method of transportation is available. Or you may want to address the way of thinking in the world that continues to support the development of more and more cars instead of cleaner, effective alternative transportation. You may address your letter to television stations that show so many advertisements promoting the excessive and unnecessary use of cars.

For example, of you were to choose the loss of old growth forests, you might examine similar audiences. You might encourage particular companies to strive less for profit or encourage governments to change policies requiring a company to cut a certain amount of wood every year to keep its license. You could address ways of living that waste wood and paper.

Remind students that these letters are to redress violations of the rights of Earth, as listed in the document they have created. The letters are being composed not so much to send to a particular person or organization (although that is a possibility), but more to address or point out the many ways in which Earth's rights are being disrespected, including the actions and thinking of large groups of people.

Step 5: After students have selected the right or rights they wish to write about and selected the target audience for the letter, ask them to select and include a statement about how they are going to contribute personally to respecting this right. What actions will they take as individuals?

Step 6: Using a guideline for writing a formal letter (either the one that follows this activity or another) and the evaluation criteria (or other criteria that reflect the focus in your class), review the requirements of a formal letter and the requirements of this specific letter.

Step 7: Allow students sufficient time to compose, revise, edit, and produce final letters. Ask them to read their letters aloud to the class. Post the letters in a visible place—hallway, foyer, or in the community. Consider submitting some to a local newspaper.

Step 8: Working individually, students copy the following phrases in their journals and complete the statements:

I think it is important to respect the rights of other life on Earth because . . .

The most effective way to encourage people to act responsibly toward Earth and its creatures is . . .

Guidelines for Writing a Formal Letter

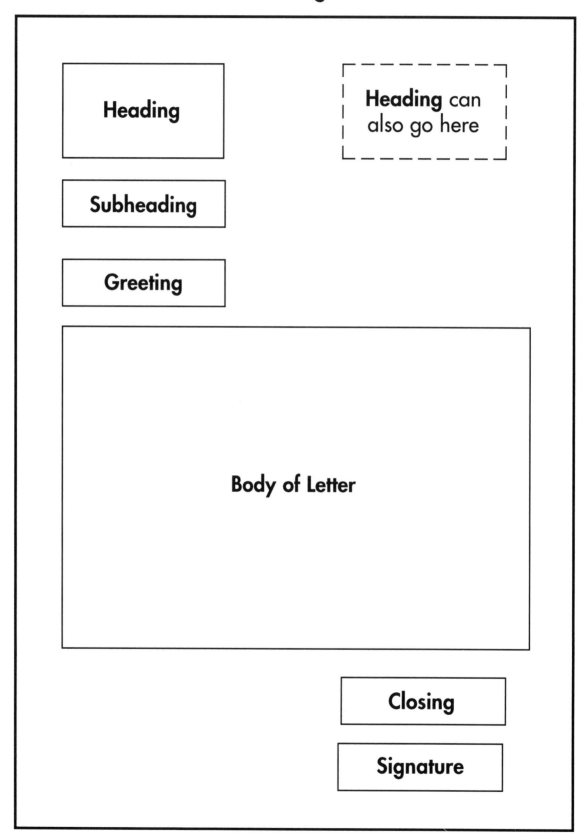

Guidelines for Writing a Formal Letter

The **HEADING** contains the date the letter is written and the complete address of the person who is sending the letter:

> April 1, 1997
> 101 Earth Avenue
> Anywhere, Oregon 00110-1010

The **SUBHEADING** contains the name and address of the person or organization who is receiving the letter:

> Mr. A. B. See, President
> Acme Consumer Co.
> Box 2288
> Somewhere, Alberta
> Canada T2B 2B1

The **GREETING** addresses the person to whom you are writing:

> Dear Mr. See,

The **BODY** of the letter includes an introduction that states the purpose for writing the letter. It explains clearly the facts. If you expect something from the person to whom you are writing, such as an action or something to be sent back to you, state your expectation. Conclude courteously.

The **CLOSING** connects the ending of the letter to your signature with a phrase such as "Yours sincerely" or "Respectfully."

The **SIGNATURE** is your handwritten name with your name typed under it if the rest of the letter is typed.

Evaluation Criteria

Activity: Letter Writing in Support of Rights of Earth

1. Letter form: contains the following parts, correctly placed and using correct punctuation and capital letters.

heading .... /3

subheading .... /3

greeting .... /3

body .... /3

closing and signature .... /3

Subtotal: .... /15

2. Letter Content

courteously worded .... /3

clearly stated purpose and facts .... /5

clearly stated expectations for change .... /5

clearly stated personal action to support this change .... /5

clearly organized sentences, according to importance .... /5

suitably stated conclusion .... /2

Subtotal .... /25

3. Quality

standard spelling, capital letters, and punctuation

neat and legible presentation .... /10

Subtotal .... /10

TOTAL .... /50

Making a Difference

Never doubt that a small group of thoughtful, committed citizens can change the world: indeed, it's the only thing that ever has.

—Margaret Mead

Sometimes it's difficult to understand or really believe that the actions and choices of one individual can make a difference. The problems seem so huge that our own efforts seem small, embarrassingly insignificant in comparison. The belief that individual acts matter is an easy target for such labels as *naive, innocent, Pollyanna-ish,* or *foolishly unaware* of the magnitude of the issues facing us. A sense of futility or pointlessness can easily develop from such thoughts and feelings. To fuel the changes in behavior and action that collectively shape the future requires the commitment and caring that knows each choice makes a difference.

This activity uses story and song to allow students to investigate and discuss how individual actions contribute to the whole and also have meaning in and of themselves.

▶ **Structure**

variable: either class, small groups, or individuals

▶ **Material**

copies of "Starfish," many variations of which are in circulation

copies of "I Really Believe"

▶ **Time**

　1 class period

▶ **Procedure**

Step 1: Read "Starfish" aloud to the class or copy it and ask students to read it individually or in pairs.

Step 2: Discuss the following questions (or other questions that you wish to pursue) as a class or in small groups, or have students respond individually in writing.

What feelings, thoughts, images, or associations come to mind when you read or heard this story?

What idea is the author expressing?

How can the main idea be applied to other areas of your life? (Or what relationship does the main idea of the story have to other areas of life or other learnings?)

If a young boy who felt the same as the old man went to the beach in the early morning and found all the stranded starfish, how would the story be different?

What do you think you would do if you were in the situation described in the story? Why?

Step 3: Read, listen to, or sing the lyrics of the song "I Really Believe" and discuss the following questions.

What thoughts, feelings, images, or associations come to mind as you read or hear the lyrics?

Compare the lyrics with the story. How are the two similar? How are they different?

What is meant by the phrase "This race can still be won."

What do you believe is the song's main idea?

Step 4: Working individually (or in a circle session), students record and complete the following phrases:

The most important thing in "Starfish" is . . .

What was most important to me in the song "I Really Believe" was . . .

The way I personally would most like to contribute to improving the situation in the world is . . .

Starfish

There had been a tremendous storm the evening before, with a wind that howled, rattling the doors and windows of the small beach cabin where the old man was staying. For most of the night he heard the huge waves crashing, driven high up the beach by the power of the unusually fierce storm.

Early in the morning, not too long before dawn, the old man listened as the wind ceased its attack on his cabin. He heard the crash of the waves grow less deafening, and finally he was able to sleep. Having come such a long way to rest and recuperate at this remote beach, such a din on his first night seemed an ironic welcome. It kept him from sleep far more insistently than the city traffic he left behind.

In spite of this loss of sleep, however, he woke early and wandered down to the beach, where the waves and wind had thrown all kinds of debris high up on the shore. The sea shone with the pale yellow of late sunrise reflected on now quiet waters.

In the distance he saw a figure, which, when he walked closer, he recognized as a young boy. The old man continued walking more slowly toward the boy, observing his actions, finally realizing that the boy was picking up starfish, one by one, and throwing them far out into the water. The waves of the previous night had thrown them far from the water. Hundreds and hundreds of them dotted the beach, which extended miles down the coast.

The old man continued walking and finally caught up to the boy. "Why are you doing that?" he asked in curiosity as the youth reached for another starfish and flung it far into the water.

"They will die here when the sun gets higher and hotter. They've been thrown too far up on the beach to survive," came the boy's response.

"But there are hundreds, maybe millions, of them. This beach goes on for miles and miles. What difference can it make?"

The young boy reached over and picked up another starfish. He held it in his hands, looked at it, and replied as he tossed it into the water, "It makes a difference to this one."

I Really Believe

Words and music by Alanda Greene

I Really Believe

Taking a look at the world today, my heart can fill with despair.
The forests are dying and burning. We've poisoned the soil and the air.
Millions of people are starving, while millions are spent on war.
Creatures are fast disappearing, and the human numbers grow more.
And at times it just seems hopeless. It seems like it's too far gone.
What is the point in even trying? Yet my heart still sings this song.

Chorus:
I really believe we can make a difference.
I really believe what we can do.
I really believe that we all matter.
There's a way to make our dreams and visions true.
I really believe it can be done.
This race can still be won.
And I'm going to join in the running,
'Cause I really believe.

Taking a look at the world today, my heart can fill with grief
For the harm we've done to our planet and I cannot see her relieved;
For the harm we've done to each other, and all of the life we share.
I wonder if it ever will heal again,
When there's so few that seem to care.
And it's easier not to face it, to pretend like there's nothing wrong.
Why bother wasting my efforts? Yet my heart still sings this song.

Chorus

Transforming Opposites

In the previous activities, students experienced differing, sometimes opposing, points of view on various issues. The diamente is a poem form particularly appropriate for expressing such opposites and for exploring the meeting ground between them or the transformation of one to another. It is an especially suitable poetic structure that allows a poem to evolve from the webbing of words and phrases, or from key word associations.

The diamente is a seven-line poem that begins and ends with single-word nouns that represent opposite ideas or positions.

Line 1: A single word, a noun

Line 2: Two words describing the noun

Line 3: Three words depicting an action linked to the noun

Line 4: Four words relating or connecting the first and last nouns

Line 5: Three words depicting an action linked to the last noun

Line 6: Two words describing the last noun

Line 7: A single word, a noun expressing the opposite of the one in line 1

The poem in the drawing (page 129) is a diamente. Following it is another one.

forest

diverse unity

ancient emerging mystery

harmony compromised profit maximized

controlled ordered replacement

numbered planting

trees

---

sky

blue space

calling reaching yearning

stars sing lilies glisten

belonging holding supporting

solid brown

earth

▶ **Structure**

individuals

▶ **Material**

paper

pencil or pen

▶ **Time**

1 class period

▶ **Procedure**

Step 1: Ask students to select, from issues examined in previous activities, two words that represent opposing views or positions. Examples include *silence* and *noise* from the flight-testing activity; *forest* and *timber* or *owls* and *logs* from the logging activity; and *harmony* and *destruction* from the visions of the future activity.

Step 2: Tell students to web or list as many word associations as they can with each of the words. Encourage them to be persistent in developing connections beyond their few immediate associations. Share examples in the class.

Step 3: Explain the structure of the diamente poem. Ask students to refer to the word lists they generated in order to write such a poem.

Step 4: Share the completed poems orally and visually, posting them where they can be read.

Bibliography

Avery, M., B. Auvine, B. Streibel, and L. Weiss. 1981. *Building United Judgment: A Handbook for Consensus Decision Making.* Madison, Wis.: Center for Conflict Resolution.

Ball, Geraldine, and Uvaldo Hill Palomares. 1977. *Magic Circle, Innerchange.* La Mesa, Calif.: Human Development Training Institute.

Brewer, Chris, and Linda Grinde, comp. 1995. *Many People, Many Ways: Understanding Cultures around the World.* Tucson, Ariz.: Zephyr Press.

Brody, E., J. Goldspinner, K. Green, R. Leventhal, and J. Porcino, eds. 1992. *Spinning Tales, Weaving Hope: Stories of Peace, Justice and the Environment.* Philadelphia: New Society Publishers.

Campbell, Bruce, Linda MacRae-Campbell, and Micki McKisson. 1992. *The Energy Crisis.* Tucson, Ariz.: Zephyr Press.

Enloe, Walter, ed. 1996. *Creating Context: Experiencing and Understanding Cultural Worlds.* Tucson, Ariz.: Zephyr Press.

Enloe, Walter, and Ken Simon, eds. 1993. *Linking through Diversity: Practical Classroom Activities for Experiencing and Understanding Our Cultures.* Tucson, Ariz.: Zephyr Press.

Fleisher, Paul. 1993. *Changing Our World: A Handbook for Young Advocates.* Tucson, Ariz.: Zephyr Press.

Hoose, Phillip. 1993. *It's Our World, Too! Stories of Young People Who Are Making a Difference.* Boston: Little, Brown.

Johnson, R, D. Johnson, and Edythe Johnson. 1987. *Structuring Cooperative Learning: Lesson Plans for Teachers.* Edina, Minn.: Interaction Book Company.

Kohn, Alfie. 1990. *The Brighter Side of Human Nature, Altruism and Empathy in Everyday Life.* New York: Basic Books.

MacRae-Campbell, Linda, and Micki McKisson. 1990a. *Our Troubled Skies.* Tucson, Ariz.: Zephyr Press.

———. 1990b. *War: The Global Battlefield.* Tucson, Ariz.: Zephyr Press.

MacRae-Campbell, Linda, Micki McKisson, and Bruce Campbell. 1990. *The Ocean Crisis.* Tucson, Ariz.: Zephyr Press.

Make a World of Difference: Creative Activities for Global Learning. 1990. New York: Friendship Press.

McKisson, Micki, and Linda MacRae-Campbell. 1990a. *Endangered Species: Their Struggle to Survive.* Tucson, Ariz.: Zephyr Press.

———. 1990b. *The Future of Our Tropical Rainforests.* Tucson, Ariz.: Zephyr Press.

———. 1990c. *Our Divided World: Poverty, Hunger, and Overpopulation.* Tucson, Ariz.: Zephyr Press.

Myers, Norman, ed. 1984. *Gaia: An Atlas of Planet Management.* Garden City, N.Y.: Doubleday, Anchor.

Myers, Robert E. 1994. *Facing the Issues: Creative Strategies for Probing Critical Social Concerns.* Tucson, Ariz.: Zephyr Press.

Myers, Robert E., and E. Paul Torrance. 1994. *What Next? Futuristic Scenarios for Creative Problem Solving.* Tucson, Ariz.: Zephyr Press.

Nelson, Annabelle. 1994. *The Learning Wheel: Ideas and Activities for Multicultural and Holistic Lesson Planning.* Tucson, Ariz.: Zephyr Press.

Pike, Graham, and David Selby. 1988. *Global Teacher, Global Learner.* London: Hodder and Stoughton.

Ruggieri-Vande Putte, Katherine. 1995. *Our Town: A Community Simulation of Contemporary Issues.* Tucson, Ariz.: Zephyr Press.

Scher, Anna, and Charles Verrall. 1975. *100+ Ideas for Drama.* London: Heinemann.

Selwyn, Douglas. 1993. *Living History in the Classroom: Integrative Arts Activities for Making Social Studies Meaningful.* Tucson, Ariz.: Zephyr Press.

Sobel, David. 1993. *Children's Special Places: Exploring the Role of Forts, Dens, and Bush Houses in Middle Childhood.* Tucson, Ariz.: Zephyr Press.

Stanford, Gene. 1977. *Developing Effective Classroom Groups: A Practical Guide for Teachers.* New York: Hart.

Tarlington, Carole, and Patrick Verriour. 1983. *Offstage: Elementary Education through Drama.* Toronto: Oxford University Press.

Wade, Rahima Carol. 1991. *Joining Hands: From Personal to Planetary Friendship in the Primary Classroom.* Tucson, Ariz.: Zephyr Press.

Wilson, Leslie Owen. 1994. *Every Child, Whole Child: Classroom Activities for Unleashing Natural Abilities.* Tucson, Ariz.: Zephyr Press.

Notes

Notes

Notes

Experiences that involve students from around the world . . .

CREATING CONTEXT

Experiencing and Understanding Cultural Worlds
Edited by Walter Enloe

Teacher's resource

Immerse your students in context to help them construct meaning and gain deeper understanding. By providing immersion experiences you'll involve all of your students' intelligences!

   Look to *Creating Context* for a collection of first-rate examples of immersion experiences develped by creative educators. You'll find more than 14 encompassing experiences that involve students from around the world.

224 pages, 7" x 10", softbound

1066-W . . . $29

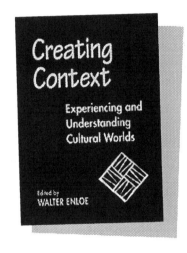

LINKING THROUGH DIVERSITY

Practical Classroom Methods for Experiencing and Understanding Our Cultures
Edited by Walter Enloe and Ken Simon

For teachers of grades K–12

   You can develop whole-minded students who are interested in the world and confident enough to interact with it. Through art exchanges, computer links, student videotapes, and other methods, you can bring the world into your classroom.

192 pages, 6" x 9", softbound

1038-W . . . $21.95